Eugène

BOUDIN

Translation Mark Hutchinson

Note

The following rules have been adopted for the catalogue entries:
— Exhibitions quoted refer to the list on page 189. In the catalogue entries themselves, only the place and date are given.
— Bibliographical data refer to the bibliography on page 188. In the catalogue entries themselves, only the author's name and the year of publication are given, with the exception of Laurent Manoeuvre, where titles are given to distinguish between two works published in 1991.
References to works not listed in the bibliography are given in full.

© Musée Eugène Boudin, Honfleur—Somogy Éditions d'Art, Paris, 1996

ISBN 2-85056-265-3
Printed in Italy

Copyright registration: fourth quarter 1996

Eugène BOUDIN

Paintings and drawings

Catalogue raisonné
Musée Eugène Boudin
Honfleur

Anne-Marie Bergeret-Gourbin
with the participation of Laurent Manœuvre

Société des Amis du Musée   Eugène Boudin Honfleur

SOMOGY
ÉDITIONS
D'ART

A rousing tribute must be payed to all those who have helped make the Musée Eugène Boudin an important centre for 19th-century painting in Normandy.

Thanks to the efforts made by successive town councils, the great generosity shown by patrons, the associative activities of the Society of Friends and the efficiency of the museum's curator, a number of important works have been acquired. The exhibitions it organises and a wide range of publications have made the museum known throughout France.

The museum as it is today also gives voice to the council's ambitions for high-level cultural events that will find echoes not only in France but abroad. A series of major exhibitions in the near future are proof of this.

But let us not forget our friend, the great painter Eugène Boudin, whose magic brush has taught people to appreciate the beaches, skies and landscapes of Normandy.

It is always a pleasure, a secret joy to meet up with him once again at the museum.

Françoise ROUSSEAU
Assitant-Mayor for Culture and Tourism, Honfleur

The Society of Friends of the Musée Eugène Boudin celebrates its fortieth anniversary this year. It was founded in 1956 by the painters Jean Driès, the museum's first curator, Fernand Herbo and André Hambourg, and by Mme Katia Granoff, under the presidency of M. Maurice Guyot. Their wish was to promote and enrich the museum's collections and thereby make them better known.

In 1971, with the aid of an important donation by the president, Mme Marcel Schlumberger, the museum's delapidated premises were enlarged and renovated under the supervision of the architect Félix Gatier. Honfleur today possesses a museum that is worthy of its collections. In 1977, Mme Geneviève Seydoux took over from her mother as president and greatly extended the activities of the museum to include posters, catalogues, post-cards, printed scarves and the acquisition of new works. A great many donations, paintings, old toys and objects have now been added to the collection.

In 1992, the Society was approved by the French state and today numbers 320 members under the presidency of Simon Chaye. The aim of the Society is the same as it was in 1956: to help our curator, Mme Anne-Marie Bergeret, acquire new works, oversee its many publications, encourage donations and make the museum known.

This new catalogue of works by the painter Eugène Boudin now preserved in the museum is the result of close collaboration between the museum and the Society of Friends. It is also the occasion to celebrate our 40th anniversary with the wish that the museum's reputation continue to grow both in France and abroad.

Simon CHAYE
President of the Society of Friends
of the Musée Eugène Boudin

Foreword

For more than fifteen years now, the Society of Friends of the Musée Eugène Boudin has been publishing catalogues of the museum's permanent collections and exhibitions. The first general guide and catalogue was published in 1983 and was reprinted, further enriched, in 1988 and 1993. The Society of Friends is a patron of the arts and helps raise public awareness of works belonging to the museum.

There was an urgent need for a *catalogue raisonné* of Eugène Boudin's works housed in the museum, which the Society of Friends has chosen to publish in association with a specialist in the field. The museum today possesses eighty-nine works by Boudin; that is to say, forty-two paintings, twenty-eight pastels, and nineteen gouaches, watercolours and pencil drawings. It is the third largest public collection of Boudin's work after the rich collections of the Musée d'Orsay and the Département des Arts Graphiques du Louvre et du Musée d'Orsay (6,400 drawings and oils on paper) and that of the Musée des Beaux-Arts du Havre (225 paintings and 68 drawings).

The collection has been built up over the years with the aid of donors, and this catalogue is a tribute to their generosity. Between 1898 and 1899, Eugène Boudin bequeathed to the museum fifty-three works which, as his executor Gustave Cahen tells us, he had carefully put aside for his native town. Though many of these works are small and represent only part of his rich career as an artist, they illustrate moments of importance or intimacy in his life.

We have chosen to classify the works by theme, for this is how Boudin himself liked to arrange his drawings in portfolios, but have respected their chronological order and placed each subject in a broad context designed to take account of its importance in Boudin's life. At the same time, we have not overlooked the technical and bibliographical data that make up the scholarly apparatus of a *catalogue raisonné*. As the first *catalogue raisonné* of works by Boudin now preserved at the Musée de Honfleur, there will necessarily be a number of oversights and errors.

It remains for me to thank those who helped bring this book about:

Geneviève Seydoux, whose many years as president gave a new lease of life to the Society, and whose energetic publishing and purchasing policy is today pursued by the new president, Simon Claye.

The Society's committee members, in particular its treasurer, Annick Rocque, its secretary, Jacqueline Lacaille, and Raymond Lacaille, who enabled us to identify the different types of wood on which Boudin painted.

Solange Lemaire, art-historian and honorary secretary of the Society, who has worked hard to make the Honfleur painters known to the public.

Laurent Manoeuvre, art-historian and research director at the Musées de France, who has been studying Boudin's work for many years now. His aid for the *Eugène Boudin* restrospective in Honfleur in 1992 was invaluable, and he has kindly contributed a text on Boudin and Brittany to this catalogue.

Claude Draeger, chairman and managing director of Éditions Anthèse, who has granted us permission to reprint certain texts published with his collaboration for the *Eugène Boudin at Honfleur* exhibition in 1992.

We would like to thank the following public bodies for their support: the French Ministère de la Culture (Direction des Musées de France and Direction Régionale des Affaires Culturelles de Basse-Normandie) and the Conseil Régional de Basse-Normandie.

Anne-Marie BERGERET-GOURBIN
Curator of the Musée Eugène Boudin.

CHRONOLOGICAL ACCOUNT OF THE MUNICIPAL MUSEUM

On 11 April 1868, the town council discussed setting up a Musée des Beaux-Arts in Honfleur. The museum opened its doors on 15 February, 1869, and remains open to the public every Sunday between 1 and 4 pm. The initiative for the museum came from Louis-Alexandre Dubourg (1821–1891), a painter from Honfleur who devoted all of his energies to his native town. The son of a naval blacksmith, Dubourg had studied in Paris in the studio of Léon Cogniet and, for a short time, taught drawing at the college of Pont-Audemer. Dubourg was assisted in his project by Gustave Morin, a painter and curator at the Musée des Beaux-Arts de Rouen who secured a few paintings for the museum. A collector and painter from Rouen, Victor Delamare, loaned fourteen paintings that he later bequeathed to the museum. Dubourg rapidly obtained support from his Honfleur friends, Eugène Boudin and Gustave Hamelin, who donated a number of small works to form the basis of the collection, which was further enriched by loans from the French state. By the time it opened, the museum could boast some fifty works.

Though Boudin was present when the museum was first created, his initial reaction to Dubourg's project was far from enthusiastic: 'he's got it into his head to waste time setting up a museum in Honfleur! That boy narrows his field too much. . .'. After this initial outburst of petulance, Boudin's friendship for Dubourg forced his interest and he thought of the future of the museum by putting it down in his will. He also put aside a number of works destined for the museum. So it was that, in 1899, in accordance with Boudin's wishes, Gustave Cahen, his executor, offered the museum fifty-three works by the painter and seventeen by his friends from Normandy, among whom Hamelin, Charles Pécrus, Antoine Vollon, Théodule Ribot and Louis Mettling.

Boudin always maintained sentimental ties with Honfleur and the artistic figures of the day. In 1896, a group of worthies founded the Société d'Ethnographie et d'Art Populaire, 'Le Vieux Honfleur'. They appealed to Eugène Boudin, who agreed to sit on the steering committee and recalled the past for them. Out of this initiative and the enthusiasm shown by the painter Léon Leclerc, the Musée d'Ethnographie was born, in the rue de la Prison where it can still be found today. At the end of the century, the Municipal Museum was run by Leclerc, who watched over the destinies of Honfleur's two museums. In an auction, the town council acquired more than a hundred of Dubourg's drawings, as a tribute to his devotion and his qualities as an artist.

The vocation of the Musée des Beaux-Arts de Honfleur was established: it was to be a museum for that pre-Impressionist painting which saw the light of day in the Seine estuary and blossomed in the years 1855–1865 around the figures of Dubourg, Boudin, Monet and Jongkind. Donations and acquisitions have since confirmed that choice, opening the museum's collections to 20th-century artists who, inspired by Honfleur and its surroundings, have prolonged or reconsidered the heritage of their elders. Thanks to the creation of the FRAM (Fonds Régional d'Acquisition pour les Musées) in 1982, the Municipal Museum, which is now the Musée Eugène Boudin, has been enriched by a large number of works designed to complete the picture of the 19th century as seen through Normandy — works by Dubourg, Pécrus, Adolphe-Félix Cals, Hamelin, Paul Huet, Louis Cabat, Camille Flers, Charles Lapostolet, Vallotton and Courbet.

The museum wishes to recreate the artistic environment of the 19th century and recover the spirit described by journalists of the last century at the Saint-Siméon Inn. Articles from 1859 and 1865, and the recollections of painters such as Amédée Besnus, told of the fellowship of the artists who would meet at the Saint-Siméon Inn, and who would leave traces of their reveries and painters' jokes on the walls of their rooms.

In 1859, a journalist advised the landlady of the inn, Mme Toutain, to acquire 'an oblong album-ledger containing some hundred sheets of different shades, about forty centimeters long by thirty centimeters wide; this album, firmly bound with copper edgings like the ledger of a business house, could be placed in a spot in the house so that it

Jacques Despierre
Portrait of Eugène Boudin
Medal (obverse)

Cat. II

Jacques Despierre
Three-Master at Anchor
Medal (reverse)

CAT. II

1. *Echo Honfleurais,* 3 September, 1859, quoted in
Honfleur avant l'Impressionnisme, exhibition catalogue,
Musée Eugène Boudin, Honfleur, 1991.

was always on hand for people able to write or sketch in it. Without any doubt, after a certain lapse of time this album would be extremely valuable. In this way, many transient works that the view of the sea and the green countryside of our region had inspired in illustrious men in Literature and the Arts would be preserved.'[1]

His advice, alas, was all to no avail, and it fell to the Musée Eugène Boudin to take up the challenge and tell the story of what is misleadingly known as 'the Saint-Siméon school'. In a constant dialogue between Eugène Boudin and his friends, the museum presents those 'transient works' inspired by 'the view of the sea and the green countryside of our region'.

Originally housed at the Hôtel de Ville, in 1924 the museum's collections were transferred by Leclerc to the chapel of the disused convent of the Augustinian nuns. The museum was inaugurated there on 8 June, 1924. Fifty years later, on 1 June, 1974, a modern museum built in line with the restored chapel was opened. It is here, in two large rooms with a wide bay-window looking out over the estuary, that the painting collections are housed, while a darker room preserves the rich Norman ethnographic collection bequeathed by a resident of Honfleur, Désiré Louveau.

In December 1988, a new extension allowed the museum to relocate various 19th-century works, set up the new Hambourg-Rachet donation and provide a show-case for its works on paper. Further modifications are currently being considered and donations prepared. The museum's purchasing policy, with strong support from the Society of Friends, is a sign of its vitality and its determination to take part in regional and national cultural policy. In 1995, the new Norman ethnographic collection bequeathed by Marie-Thérèse and Marcel Legrand confirmed the interest shown by art-lovers and collectors in the museum, thereby establishing its deep commitment to the arts in Normandy.

CHRONOLOGICAL ACCOUNT OF WORKS BY EUGÈNE BOUDIN added to the museum's collections between 1868 and 1996

This list also includes iconographic material concerning Eugène Boudin (cat. I to XIII).

1892. Bequest by Louis-Alexandre Dubourg, a friend of Eugène Boudin and founder of the museum, of a painting (cat. 45).

1899. Bequest by Eugène Boudin to his native town of fifty-three of his own works, that is twenty-nine paintings and twenty-four pastel drawings, and sixteen paintings from his private collection. The bequest was carried out by his executor Gustave Cahen, a lawyer from Paris.
On 8 August, 1898, Cahen announced to the mayor of Honfleur:

'Monsieur le Maire,
The painter Eugène Boudin, native of your town, has just died this morning in Deauville where he had wished to be conveyed.
In my capacity as Eugène Boudin's executor, I can inform you at once that my friend has bequeathed a considerable number of paintings to your town. I am alerting the administration of the Beaux-Arts and going to Paris to attend to the funeral of Eugène Boudin, who has a vault in the cemetery at Montmartre.
I hope the municipality of Honfleur will wish to join in the mourning caused by the death of this great artist who, in his last wishes, proved himself an affectionate and grateful son to his native town'.

In a letter to the mayor on 9 August, Cahen added: 'Today, I have left at the court his will, in which he bequeaths to your town a considerable number of paintings that he always refused to sell and that I knew were intended for you'. This fully confirms the sentimental value Boudin attached to these works, over and above their anecdotal appearance as small beach scenes, portraits and so forth. It is now clear that the small figure studies are of his father, his wife Marie-Anne and his sister-in-law; and that one of the beach scenes, *The Conversation* (cat. 79), is, in fact, the *Light Meal* in company with his friend, the painter Mettling.

The bequest comprised twenty-five shares with an estimated value of 2,050 francs. The painting to which the highest estimate was attached was n° 21, *Still-life with Fowl* (cat. 11): 250 francs, while one of the beach scenes was valued at 150 francs. N° 23 comprised four small portraits. The first works offered to the museum were those by Boudin's friends Hamelin, Pécrus (including a portrait of Marie-Anne Boudin, cat. VIII), Mettling (including a portrait of Boudin, cat. V), Ribot, Henri Michel-Lévy (including a portrait of Boudin paintings cows near the river Touques, cat. VI) and Frédéric Thorin. The pastel drawings were later added to this first list of paintings.

1899. Gift by Louis Boudin, the painter's brother, of a painting (cat. 61). Boudin always remained on very good terms with his brother Louis, as is shown by their correspondence. Louis, in turn, was devoted to his brother's memory and offered the town of Le Havre '60 canvases and 180 panels' from the contents of the artist's studio, along with a large number of drawings (over six thousand) currently preserved at the Département des Arts Graphiques du Louvre et du Musée d'Orsay.

1900. Purchase by the Ville de Honfleur of a bust of Eugène Boudin (cat. III), commissioned from the sculptor Ernest Guilbert (1848–after 1913), who specialised in effigies of figures drawn from history (Étienne Dolet, Adolphe Thiers, Christopher Columbus, Eugène Delacroix) or mythology (Daphnis and Chloe, Themis).
Gustave Cahen had proposed setting up a bust in Honfleur in memory of Boudin at the entrance to the former west jetty. Sculpted in marble by Ernest-Charles Guilbert, the bust was set on a plinth adorned with the palette and palm of fame, the attributes of the well-known painter. The cost of 8,000 francs was met by a subscription involving the French state (500 fr.), art-lovers (4,000 fr.), the town (500 fr.), 'Le Vieux Honfleur', Boudin's family and his last companion, Juliette Cabaud (2,000 fr.?).
The inauguration, held on 8 July, 1900, was the occasion for regattas, and M. Albert Sorel delivered the opening speech. The Ministre de l'Instruction Publique et des Beaux-Arts delegated M. Roger Marx,

Inspecteur Général des Musées des Départements, to preside over the ceremony. A bronze version of the bust can still be seen in the public garden at Honfleur, while the patinated plaster-cast is kept at the Musée Eugène Boudin.

1900. Gift by Gustave Cahen of a dry-point engraving (cat. IV) by Paul Helleu (1859–1927). This dry-point engraving was the frontispiece for the numbered edition of Cahen's *Eugène Boudin, sa Vie et son Oeuvre,* published in 1900.
Helleu often visited Trouville on his yacht and in 1894 made three dry-point engravings of Boudin painting near the jetties. Helleu was a friend of Monet's who admired Boudin and was particularly fond of his pastel studies of skies. He acquired eight of these, including two studies formerly belonging to Corot.

1934. Gift by Boudin's friend, the composer Georges Sporck, of two pastel drawings and a photograph of Boudin painting near the jetties at Trouville in June 1896, dedicated to Georges Sporck (cat. 30, 31 and I). Sporck was the son of Jules Sporck, a Paris manufacturer of furniture trimmings and friend of Boudin and Corot (R. Schmit, 1973, vol. 1).

1937. Gift by Désiré Louveau of five paintings. Louveau was born in Honfleur in 1843 and was a wine merchant, local scholar and founder member of 'Le Vieux Honfleur'. He performed a great many social functions, including that of town councillor, judge at the commercial court, founder of the tourist office and administrator of a variety of charitable and educational organisations.

1954. Bequest by Adrien Voisard-Margerie, painter and curator of the museum from 1930 to 1953, of a large painting, *Port of Dieppe* (cat. 86), offered to him by Madame Louveau.
Gift of a portrait painted by Voisard-Margerie from a photograph of Boudin reproduced for the 1908 exhibition at the Grand Palais in Paris (cat. IX).

1956. Gift by Michel Monet of two paintings by Claude Monet and two drawings, one of which is thought to be a portrait of Boudin working at Le Havre (cat. VII)

1959. Gift by Pablo Ispenian of a painting, *The Trouville Road* (cat. 57), in memory of Jean Hallaure, a man of letters from Le Havre.

1959. Gift by Mme Katia Granoff of the painting, *Cows in the Touques Valley* (cat. 69). Around 1959, Katia Granoff opened a gallery on the quai Sainte-Catherine (then known as the quai Saint-Étienne) in Honfleur, where it can still be found. The quality of this generous lady's gifts to the museum — which include works by Georges-Michel, Eugène Isabey and Courbet — has played a large part in enriching its collections.

1963. Gift by Mme Katia Granoff of *Still-Life with Skate* (cat. 7).

1966. Gift of two pencil drawings (cat. 15 and 16) by Dr. Georges Bréhier, founder member, then honorary president of the Society of Friends of the Musée Eugène Boudin, and former mayor of Honfleur.

1974. Loan by 'Le Vieux Honfleur' of a small portable easel formerly owned by Boudin (cat. XI).

1974. Gift of one of the artist's palettes (cat. XIII) by Jean Fischer, an English teacher at the Collège de Honfleur and amateur painter, taught by Henri de Saint-Delis. Fischer was one of the key figures of the Société des Artistes Honfleurais.

1974. Gift by the painter, Jacques Despierre, of a medal (cat. XII) representing Boudin on the obverse and large sailing boats on the reverse.

1977. Gift of two letters from Eugène Boudin to Jehan Soudan de Pierrefitte, 3 August and 25 October, 1896 (including the letter of the 'legend' of Saint-Siméon, cat. 46). Gift made by Mme Maurice

Guyot in memory of her husband, who was president and founder of the Society of Friends of the Musée de Honfleur (founded in 1956) and Secrétaire Général of the Sorbonne for thirty-five years.

1979. Bequest by M. and Mme Marest-Devillers of a pencil drawing (cat. 17). André Marest taught French and philosophy for thirty-seven years at the Lycée Albert Sorel in Honfleur. Mme Thérèse Marest, née Devillers was a Honfleur poetess and school-teacher, and a friend of Lucie Delarue-Mardrus.

1988. Important donation by Nicole Hambourg-Rachet and André Hambourg, including eighteen works by Boudin (seventeen drawings and a painting) and a portfolio. Sixteen of these works came from the collection of Dr. Pierre-Armand Rachet, and two drawings from that of André Hambourg. Pierre-Armand Rachet (1856–1926) was a doctor who settled in Honfleur where, for thirty years, he was a town councillor and Médecin-Chef at the Hospice de Honfleur. He was also a trade-union activist and mutualist. His profession brought him into contact with Boudin, whose sketches and studies he loved and collected, filing them away in portfolios. He also surrounded himself with works by 'estuary painters' (Dubourg, Emile Renouf, Adolphe Marais and others).

1989. Gift of a watercolour *Women on the Beach at Berck* (cat. 90) by René Küss, Emeritus Professor at the Université de Paris, former President of the Académie de Médecine, former President of the Société des Artistes Honfleurais and member of the board of directors of the Society of Friends of the Musée Eugène Boudin.

1990. Gift of a painting *Trouville, Entrance to the Jetties at Low Tide* (cat. 72) by Jacques Boussard, a painter and member of the board of directors of the Society of Friends of the Musée Eugène Boudin. In making this gesture, he wished to honour a painter he loved and to enrich a museum that he frequented and whose activities he supported.

BIOGRAPHY

Boudin travelled widely in France, Belgium, the Netherlands and Italy. In France, he made regular visits to Picardy, the Pas de Calais, Bordeaux and the Midi. It was in his native Normandy, however, and in Brittany, the home of his wife, that he made his most frequent and lengthy stays. The following biography does not mention all his many comings and goings, but provides a summary of his existence as man and painter, his friendships, difficulties and achievements.

1824. 12 July. Birth of Eugène Boudin in the rue Bourdet in Honfleur, son of Léonard-Sébastien Boudin and Marie-Félicité Buffet.

1835. The Boudin family settles at 51 Grand Quai, Le Havre.

1836. After a year at the École des Frères des écoles chrétiennes, Boudin works as an assistant to the printer, Joseph Morlent, then to the stationer Alphonse Lemasle.

1838. Boudin's father works as a seaman on 'Le Français', a steamship operating between Le Havre and Honfleur (where he remains until 1862). Boudin's mother works as a maid on the Le Havre-Rouen link, before joining the Compagnie des Bateaux de Honfleur.

1844. Boudin opens a stationer's in Le Havre, in partnership with Jean Acher.

1845. Millet, on his way through Le Havre, sees Boudin's early works.

1846. Boudin 'buys off' someone to replace him for his military service and breaks off his partnership with Acher.

1847. Stays in Paris.

1849. In August, at the request of Baron Taylor, Boudin travels through northern France and Belgium to sell tickets for a national subscription scheme for writers and artists in need. He takes advantage of the trip to visit the museums.

The house where Boudin was born

Opposite :
Charles Pécrus
Portrait of Marie-Anne Boudin
1879

Cat. VIII

Baudelaire's house

1851. 6 February. The town council of Le Havre awards Boudin a scholarship of 1,200 francs to study painting for a year in Paris. Boudin's request was supported by Thomas Couture and Constant Troyon.
24 July. Enrolls at the Louvre as *élève copiste*.
Between 1850 and 1860, Boudin stays regularly in Paris, while continuing to live in Le Havre and Honfleur.

1855. Summer. First trip to Finistère, which he visits regularly between 1865 and 1876.

1856. First mention in Boudin's diary of Marie-Anne Guédès, born in 1835 in Rusaden, near Hanvec.

1857. 14 July. Boudin attends the *pardon* of Sainte-Anne-la-Palud, the subject of the first painting he sends to the Salon in 1859.

1858. Meets Monet in Gravier's shop in Le Havre (Gravier was the brother-in-law of Jean Acher, his former associate). They paint together on the outskirts of Le Havre where Monet discovers colour.

1859. 15 April. Salon: n° 230, *The Pardon of Sainte-Anne-la-Palud, at the Far End of the Baie de Douarnenez.*
April. Baudelaire is in Honfleur where he writes a review of the Salon and speaks very highly of Boudin's pastels that he had seen at the artist's home in Honfleur.
16 June. Courbet visits Honfleur.

1861. February. Boudin is in Paris, at 66, rue Pigalle. Works with Troyon. Continues to rent a house in Honfleur.

1862. September. Jongkind stays in Trouville and Honfleur, where the two men meet.

1863. 14 January. Marriage of Eugène Boudin and Marie-Anne Guédès in Le Havre.

13 February. Ferdinand Martin coins the term *'élégantes'* in speaking of the beach-scenes Boudin has been painting at Trouville since 1860.
3 June. Death of Boudin's father in Le Havre.

1864. September. Boudin is in Trouville, Courbet in Deauville, Monet and Jongkind in Honfleur (where Boudin joins them).

1865. Death of Troyon.
August–November. Courbet is in Trouville with Whistler.
Boudin now has rented accommodation in Trouville. Though a resident of Paris and Trouville, he continues to travel regularly, notably in Brittany during the summer.
Since 1864, his income has been improving.

1868. July. Takes part in the *Exposition Maritime du Havre,* after arranging for Courbet, Manet and Monet to send paintings.

1869. 23 May. Visits Henri Harpignies, 'one of the skilled, who should give me a few good notions' of watercolour.

1870. After staying in Normandy and Brittany, Boudin embarks for Dunkerque on 7 December, and on 12 December is in Brussels, where he meets up with Vollon and Diaz de la Pena.

1871. 8 June. Death of Boudin's mother in Le Havre.
Starts suffering from neuralgia.
September. Boudin is in Brittany.
1 December. Returns to Paris.

1872. Continues to see Monet and corresponds with Courbet, exiled after the Commune.
Summer in Trouville and Brittany.
His income has risen sharply (17,325 francs in 1872, as against 4,420 francs in 1869).

Claude Monet
Eugène Boudin Working at Le Havre
Thought to be an early portrait

Cat. VII

Eugène Boudin's palette
c. 1874

Cat. xiii

1873. August. Visits Berck.
October–November. Visits Bordeaux for the first time.

1874. Takes part in the first Impressionist exhibition at Nadar's gallery at 35 boulevard des Capucines in Paris.

1875. Travels in northern France — Berck, Boulogne, Calais — 'for a change of motifs', then in Holland.
Death of Millet and Corot.

1875–1880. Income falls again (between 2,000 and 7,000 francs a year).

1878. Death of Courbet.

1881. Business picks up, Boudin's 'time and energy [being] completely taken up by [Paul] Durand-Ruel', the dealer who was to make him known on the other side of the Atlantic.

1883. 1 February. Exhibition of 150 paintings and drawings to inaugurate the new premises of the Galerie Durand-Ruel at 9 boulevard de la Madeleine in Paris.
1 May. *Médaille de seconde classe* at the Salon.

1884. January. Presides over a banquet in honour of Théodule Ribot.
Low Tide purchased at the Salon by the French state and placed on loan at the Musée de Saint-Lô.
Decides to build a house in the rue Oliffe in Deauville.

1885. First trip to the Midi. Stays there every winter from 1890 to 1898, so as to continue painting in the open air despite problems with his health.

1886. Second painting purchased at the Salon by the French state, *A Seed*, placed on loan at the Musée de Morlaix.

1887. Exhibition of Boudin's works in America, thanks to Durand-Ruel.

1889. 24 March. Death of Marie-Anne Boudin in Paris.
8 July. *Boudin–Desboutin* exhibition at the Galerie Durand-Ruel in Paris. Urged on by Puvis de Chavannes, Boudin joins the future Société Nationale des Beaux-Arts, which has seceded from the Salon des Artistes Français.

1890. December. Durand-Ruel exhibits ninety-nine paintings and pastel drawings by Boudin and buys fifty-two paintings from him in the course of the year.

1891. Death of Jongkind and Boudin's friend from Honfleur, Louis-Alexandre Dubourg, founder of the Musée des Beaux-Arts de Honfleur (the future Musée Eugène Boudin).
June. *Boudin–Renoir* exhibition at the Galerie Durand-Ruel.
15 September. Death of *'l'ami Ribot'*.

1892. February. Trip to the Midi (Villefranche, Nice, Beaulieu, Antibes) and first trip to Venice.
July–August. Exchange of letters between Boudin and Monet. The latter writes to him on 22 August: 'I haven't forgotten that it was you who first taught me to see and understand'.
2 November. Puvis de Chavannes presents Boudin with the insignia of the Chevalier de la Légion d'Honneur.

1894. Takes up with 'Juliette' (Cabaud), who was to remain with him up until his death.

1897. 'Pilgrimages' in Brittany and Normandy. Wages a 'campaign' in Honfleur: La Lieutenance, the port, the lighthouse, the market.

1898. 27 April. Boudin writes to his brother Louis: 'For months I've been unable to tolerate solid food and my only sustenance has been two litres of

Antoine Vollon
Portrait (thought to be of Juliette)
n. d.

CAT. X

26

Ernest-Charles Guilbert
Bust of Eugène Boudin
1900

Cat. III

milk a day . . . I no longer paint, I no longer have the strength nor the desire'.

8 August. Boudin dies at six in the morning in his home in Deauville. He is buried in the cemetery of Saint-Vincent-de-Montmartre.

The only painting he dates this year is *The Baie des Fourmis at Beaulieu* (Schmit 3651, private collection).

1899. January. Exhibition at the École des Beaux-Arts: 125 paintings, 99 watercolours and 57 pastels.

20–21 March. Auction at the Hôtel Drouot of 275 of Boudin's works. Bequest to his native town of fifty-three of his own works and seventeen works by his friends Hamelin, Pécrus and Ribot.

1900. 8 July. Inauguration in Honfleur of a bust of Eugène Boudin by the sculptor Ernest-Charles Guilbert. The bust was originally placed on the western jetty, but now stands in the public garden near the estuary and the main jetty.

1 Copies

Boudin's activity in this field is borne out by his writings and account books. Only a few of Boudin's copies have been recorded to date:[1] seven paintings and a number of pencil or pastel drawings preserved at the Musée Eugène Boudin, the Musée des Beaux-Arts du Havre and in private collections. Some copies mentioned by Boudin have not been found, but may have survived unidentified in private collections.

From 1847 to 1853, Boudin made copies of the Old Masters for a handful of art-lovers, among whom M. Taylor of Le Havre. Boudin took a certain pleasure in performing bread-and-butter work of this kind, for he believed in looking at the elders, who, in his view, had 'the genius to enchant'.[2] He expressed this view in a letter to his brother Louis in 1847, repeating it to his friend Ferdinand Martin in 1869 and to Louis Braquaval in 1895. To Louis Boudin, he confided how, when lost 'in the middle of this great city [Paris], there are only the cafés and restaurants to fall back on . . . I prefer to put the day to good account copying a Ruisdael. I shan't be bringing back many studies, as I've looked more than I've carried out, but I'll have made the most of what I've seen'.[3] To Martin, Boudin recommended trying his hand at a few sketches after beautiful Flemish paintings.[4] He likewise advised Braquaval to see the Old Masters, particularly the Dutch.[5] In 1849, he took advantage of a trip to Belgium to visit the Musée de Tournai and the cathedral there, with its painting by Van Dyck. He was struck by the latter and analysed in a portrait 'the purplish forehead that is the seat of thought— the half-tones are so combined that one feels them turning on its ground — the tone is a pale lemon yellow with an admixture of violet'.[6] In Le Havre, Taylor gave him an opportunity to earn a little money, by commissioning, on 14 November, 1849, copies of *Travellers' Resting Place* by Van Ostade and paintings by Nicolas Lancret and Joseph Vernet. But Taylor wanted real copies, properly finished works.[7] Boudin's account books for the years 1850–1860 reveal that, on 6 January 1853, he delivered Taylor a copy of Van Goyen, and, on 20 June 1853, a Ruisdael and a Cuyp for 80 francs the pair.[8]

These events show how highly Boudin thought of the painters of the Northern Schools. The copies preserved at the Musée de Honfleur and the Musée du Havre bear this out: Jacob Van Ruisdael (1628/29–1682), Adriaen Van Ostade (1610–1684), Paulus Potter (1625–1654), Adriaen van de Velde (1636–1672), Frans Snyders (1579–1657) and Melchior d'Hondecoeter (1636–1695). One of Boudin's earliest admirations, however, was an Englishman, Joshua Reynolds (1723–1792),[9] and he continued to show a marked interest in 18th-century French painting, making copies of Watteau and of a

1. Robert and Manuel Schmit, 1993.

2. Gérard Jean-Aubry, unpublished notes, private collection.

3. To Louis Boudin, 5 April, 1847 (documentation of the Musée d'Orsay).

4. To Ferdinand Martin, 14 June, 1864 (Bibliothèque d'Art et d'Archéologie, Paris).

5. To Louis Braquaval, 1 March, 1895 (private collection).

6. Gérard Jean-Aubry, unpublished notes, private collection.

7. 'If you are not otherwise occupied, you could make me a copy of *Travellers' Resting Place* by Van Ostade — and I would also like something else by Ostade to go with it, which I leave to you to choose. There are also several paintings by Lancret and Vernet that, if you do not want too high a price, I may well commission from you . . . I would like them to be real copies, properly finished' (Gérard Jean-Aubry, unpublished notes, private collection).

8. On 10 June, 1852, Boudin received 25 francs from M. Taylor 'for repairing 2 Kuyps [sic]'. On 6 January, 1853, he 'gave M. Taylor 1 copy of Van Goyen and 1 painting by [Jan] Mostaert (exchange). Received 2 Palamedes.'. On 20 June 1853, he 'sold M. Taylor 1 Ruisdael and 1 Kuyp [sic] (80 the pair). That same day, he

received 60 francs to make a copy of a work by Potter (account books, private collection).

9   4 August, 1847: 'I began by making copies after painters — Josué Reynolds [sic] was my first master' (Gérard Jean-Aubry, unpublished notes, private collection).

10 Journal, 3 August, 1847: 'I've begun working from nature, it's the great master today' (Gérard Jean-Aubry, unpublished notes, private collection).

11 *Carte de copiste* n° 1430 and 441.

12 Size of copies: *The Meadow,* 86 x 122 cm., *The Gale,* 110 x 156 cm. Size of originals: 84 x 121 cm. and 110 x 160 cm.

13 Gérard Jean-Aubry, unpublished notes, private collection.

14 Pencil studies belonging to a private collection in Normandy. See *Eugène Boudin,* exhibition catalogue, Musée Eugène Boudin, Honfleur, 1992 (n° 176, 177).

great many still-lifes by Chardin (including *The Skate*, cat. 7).

Keeping company with the Old Masters and making copies played an important part in the training of this self-taught painter. Boudin began observing the Old Masters early on in his career, but soon realised (in 1847) that observation of nature was equally indispensable to him.[10] Before devoting himself to the landscapes and seascapes for which he is famous, Boudin went off to improve himself in Paris, thanks to the scholarship he was awarded by the town of Le Havre between 1851 and 1853. In exchange for the allowance, he had to send the town works testifying to the progress he had made. He thus trained his eye by studying the elders, making copies at the Louvre of *The Meadow* by Paulus Potter and *The Gale* by Jacob van Ruisdael.[11] These two large studies then went into the collections of the Musée des Beaux-Arts du Havre.[12] Boudin also copied at the Louvre Watteau's *The Pilgrimage to Cythera* (cat. 1), a detail from *Family Portrait* by Adriaen Van Ostade (cat. 3) and *Horse-Drawn Carriage Making its Way on the Beach at Scheveningen* by Adriaen van de Velde (cat. 2), copies that are now preserved at the Musée Eugène Boudin in Honfleur. Faced with these masterpieces, Boudin expressed his modesty: *I didn't get to the Louvre until Tuesday . . . but the impression it made on me was overwhelming, one needs to work with enormous courage, I reckon, to achieve anything worthwhile after all those masterpieces. I've begun several copies: every morning we're there at eight and work almost without let until four.*[13] He also worked in Normandy at the Musée des Beaux-Arts du Havre[14] and the Musée des Beaux-Arts de Caen, where he made two small pastel drawings after two large paintings: Frans Snyders' *Interior of a Pantry* (cat. 5) and Melchior de Hondecoeter's *A Hen and Her Chicks* (cat. 4).

Analysis of the copies preserved at the Musée Eugène Boudin in Honfleur reveals how faithful the artist was to his models: composition, volumes, lighting and atmosphere are all respected. His stroke is more that of a sketch and is little concerned with detail. He doesn't linger over the exact design, but renders volumes with broad strokes. The copies Boudin produced often use smaller formats than the originals. In his little sketches after Snyders and Hondecoeter, his aim is not to bring out the lush descriptive qualities of the originals, but to inscribe the volumes and their tonal values in relation to one another. In *The Pilgrimage to Cythera,* Boudin has respected the mood of the painting and the development of the story. He leaves out none of the figures, suggests Watteau's touch and reproduces the same luminous accents on the figures. These exercises prove that, by 1850–1855, Boudin already possessed the synthetic spirit and wiry line, used to structure the subject, that are later found in the works of his maturity.

1 THE PILGRIMAGE TO CYTHERA, c. 1849

Oil on canvas, 48 x 64.5 cm.
Unsigned, n.d.
Eugène Boudin bequest, 1899 (Inv. 899-1-26)

Exhibition
1956 Galerie Katia Granoff, Paris, cat. n° 30

Bibliography
Catalogues of the Musée Eugène Boudin,
1911 (n° 35), 1959 (n° 37)
R. Schmit, 1973, vol. I, n° 22

After The Pilgrimage to Cythera *by Antoine Watteau, 1717 (oil on canvas, 129 x 194 cm., Musée du Louvre, Paris, Inv. 8325).*

Antoine Watteau
The Pilgrimage to Cythera
1717

The Pilgrimage to Cythera, c. 1849
After Antoine Watteau

Cat. 1

2 THE BEACH AT SCHEVENINGEN, c. 1851–1855

Formerly oil on paper mounted on canvas
Currently paper mounted on board,
30.8 x 40.5 cm.
Unsigned, n.d.
Eugène Boudin bequest, 1899
(Inv. 899–1–25)

Exhibitions
1956 Galerie Katia Granoff, Paris, cat. n° 49
1980 Fondation Prouvost, Marcq-en-Barœul,
cat. n° 1
1992, Musée Eugène Boudin and Grenier à
Sel, Honfleur, cat. n° 2, ill. p. 14

Bibliography
Catalogues of the Musée Eugène Boudin,
1911 (n° 34), 1959 (n° 62)
R. and M. Schmit, 1993, vol. IV, n° 3857

After studying the Dutch painters, Boudin copied Horse-Drawn Carriage Making its Way on the Beach at Scheveningen, *painted by Adriaen van de Velde in 1660 (oil on wood, 37 x 49 cm., Musée du Louvre, Paris, Inv. 1915). Boudin discovered the Netherlands rather late. He painted the beach at Scheveningen in 1875, 1876, 1879 and 1890, and, as on the beaches of Normandy and northern France, depicted fishermen and their boats.*

Adriaen van de Velde
Horse-Drawn Carriage Making its Way on the Beach at Scheveningen
1660

The Beach at Scheveningen, c. 1851–1855
After Adriaen van de Velde

Cat. 2

3 | TWO WOMEN, c. 1851–1855

Oil on poplar-wood panel, 24.3 x 18.6 cm.
Unsigned
Eugène Boudin bequest, 1899 (Inv. 899-1-27)

Exhibition
1992 Musée Eugène Boudin and Grenier à Sel,
Honfleur, cat. n° 3

Bibliography
Catalogues of the Musée Eugène Boudin,
1911 (n° 33), 1959 (n° 58)
R. Schmit, 1973, vol. I, n° 27

Copy of a detail from a painting by Adriaen van Ostade, Family Portrait *(1654, oil on wood, 70 x 88 cm., Musée du Louvre, Paris, Inv. 1679).*

Adriaen Van Ostade
Family Portrait
1654

Two Women, c. 1851–1855
After Adriaen van Ostade

4 A HEN AND HER CHICKS, c. 1854–1862

Pastel on blue-grey paper, 20.4 x 19.3 cm.
Unsigned
Eugène Boudin bequest, 1899 (Inv. 899-1-51)

Exhibitions
1958 Galerie Charpentier, Paris
1992 Musée Eugène Boudin and Grenier à Sel,
Honfleur, cat. n° 257

Bibliography
Catalogue of the Musée Eugène Boudin, 1959
(n° 36)

*Copy of a painting by Melchior
d'Hondecoeter,* A Hen and her Chicks *(oil
on canvas, 76.5 x 74 cm., Musée des Beaux-
Arts, Caen, Inv. 106).*

Melchior d'Hondecoeter
A Hen and her Chicks

A Hen and her Chicks, c. 1854–1862
After Melchior d'Hondecoeter

5 INTERIOR OF A PANTRY, c. 1854–1862

Pastel on grey-blue paper, 25 x 20 cm.
Eugène Boudin bequest, 1899. (Inv. 899-1-50)

Exhibitions
1958 Galerie Charpentier, Paris
1992 Musée Eugène Boudin and Grenier à Sel,
Honfleur, cat. n° 256 (ill. p. 19)

Bibliography
Catalogue of the Musée Eugène Boudin, 1911
(n° 167), 1959 (n° 38)

*Copy of a very large painting
by Frans Snyders,* Interior of a Pantry *(oil
on canvas, 238.8 x 227.2 cm., Musée des
Beaux-Arts, Caen, Inv. 12). Boudin's visits to
Caen are attested very early on. On 16
March, 1853, Couveley wrote to him: 'Le
Maire told me . . . that you were more often at
Caen, Rouen and Le Havre' (Gérard Jean-
Aubry, 1968, pp.16–17). In 1862, Boudin
and Dubourg organised a joint exhibition-
sale at Caen. This pastel drawing may well
have been executed during this period.*

Frans Snyders
Interior of a Pantry

Interior of a Pantry
After Frans Snyders, *c. 1854–1862*

<small>Cat. 5</small>

2 STILL-LIFES

The still-life is a theme that Boudin treated early on in his career: the main creative period is situated between 1853 and 1865, or thereabouts. One or two works are dated around 1870–1880. In 1853 and 1854, Boudin sent the town of Le Havre, which had awarded him a scholarship, two copies of Dutch paintings and a still-life. The first sale of a still-life mentioned in the artist's account books is dated February 1855. Further sales were recorded over the following years. Contrary to what was claimed by his friend Léon Berthoud,[1] who in January 1856 deplored how unsuccessful Boudin's still-lifes had been, dealers were asking Boudin not only for seascapes, but for paintings of flowers, fruit and vegetables.

Between 1856 and 1863, Boudin sold a number of still-lifes to dealers and collectors in Le Havre, whose names turn up regularly in his account books: Lebas, Favre, Lemarchand, Valls, Aubourg.[2] Boudin also exhibited and sold a great many still-lifes at exhibitions in Rouen (1856) and Le Havre (1858), and in public auctions.

At a sale in Le Havre on 10 January, 1861, ten still-lifes were sold for between 30 and 78 francs apiece.[3] The works in question were classified as 'dining-room paintings', thereby confirming the decorative purposes for which they were made. Boudin was entrusted, for example, with carrying out for the dining-room of a certain M. Bonvoisin in Montivilliers (near Le Havre) three still-lifes composed of fruit, flowers and utensils on a table.[4] At another sale in April 1862, eight still-lifes were sold for between 36 and 95 francs apiece, some of their prices being higher than those paid for beach scenes from the same period. As for the sale in Le Havre on 2 July, 1863, of the twenty-four works announced, twelve were still-lifes. This so-called 'minor' genre was appreciated by the bourgeoisie, and Boudin was responding to demand. Nevertheless, though still-lifes figure in sales in Normandy and public collections, they seem to have disappeared after 1864 or 1865. No still-lifes are mentioned in the exhibitions held at the Salon des Artistes Français or the Société Nationale des Beaux-Arts between 1859 and 1897. Likewise, no still-lifes are listed in the auction catalogue for the sale of Boudin's studio at the Hôtel Drouot on 20 and 21 March, 1899. The exhibition held at the Société Nationale des Beaux-Arts from 9 to 30 January, 1899, as a tribute to the recently deceased artist, numbered 337 items, with two still-lifes bearing symbolic witness to Boudin's early success: a still-life with fish from the Musée des Beaux-Arts du Havre, and a still-life with game that Boudin had bequeathed to the Musée de Honfleur (cat. 10).

[1] Gérard Jean-Aubry, unpublished notes, private collection.

[2] Lebas was a supplier of frames in Le Havre; Favre-Lemarchand a supplier of panels; Valls an insurance man in Le Havre; Aubourg a framer and colour merchant in Paris. All bought or sold works by Boudin (Robert Schmit, 1973, vol. I).

[3] Robert Schmit, 1973, vol. 3, p. 15.

[4] Robert and Manuel Schmit, 1993, n° 3882–3884.

This only makes the still-lifes owned by the Musée Eugène Boudin that much more interesting. They date from different periods. *Still-Life with a Leg of Lamb* (cat. 6) is thought to date from around 1859. *Crab, Lobster and Fish* (cat. 7) was part of the sale in Le Havre in 1861 and was bought by Valls for 46 francs. Two further still-lifes with fowl (cat. 10 and 11) date from 1879, when Boudin briefly returned to the theme. Finally, two large, sombre still-lifes with fish are thought to date from the 1870s (cat. 8 and 9).[5] These paintings give a clear idea of the way Boudin's technique evolved: from descriptive and sketched work, he moved towards a form of Impressionism where the rendering of bird-feathers led him to adopt long, fine, fragmented and juxtaposed brushstrokes. Effects of light and volume were suggested without having to circumscribe them with a line. Finally, these still-lifes remind us of the artist's stylistic allusions, with a nod in the direction of Chardin's *The Skate* (1728) or the observation of chiaroscuro effects of Flemish painting. Much sought-after in the 17th and 18th centuries, the still-life went into a decline under the onslaught of the glorious masters of the First Empire, but returned in force in the latter part of the 19th century in the works of realist and pre-Impressionist painters. The latter rediscovered the works of Chardin, fifteen of whose still-lifes were admitted to the Louvre between 1852 and 1869; and it was at the Louvre that young artists (Boudin in 1851–1853) studied and copied.

The generation of artists born between 1810 and 1830 — Cals, Dubourg, Ribot, Vollon, Bonvin and Courbet — created new compositions in which the symbolic interest was relinquished in favour of objective reality. They occasionally modelled their works on classical compositions — sideboards, tablecloths, carafes, glasses, baskets of fruit — while enlarging the subject-matter. And they in turn were to educate the painters of the Impressionist generation, who would make use of this theme. When, in March 1859, the town council of Le Havre received a request for a scholarship from the young Oscar-Claude Monet, the request was accompanied by a still-life. After it had been turned down by the council, Monet offered the still-life to Boudin, by way of homage. Monet was still voicing his admiration for Ribot and his compositions in 1864.[6]

In this rediscovery of a supposedly minor genre, Boudin, the *catalogue raisonné* [7] of whose works lists sixty-nine still-lifes and bouquets, played a far from negligible role in the 1850s. The different approaches he adopted to the subject over the years make him a crucial artist who united tradition and modernity.

5. They resemble a large still-life in the Musée des Beaux-Arts du Havre and may be compared to similar works carried out by a friend of Boudin's, Antoine Vollon.

6. John Rewald, *Histoire de l'Impressionnisme,* vol. I, Paris, 1971, p. 61.

7. Robert and Manuel Schmit, 1993, nos 3882–3884.

6 STILL-LIFE WITH A LEG OF LAMB, c. 1859

Oil on coarse-grained canvas, 22.3 x 35.5 cm.
Unsigned, n.d.
Eugène Boudin bequest, 1899 (Inv. 899-1-20)

Exhibitions
1953 Mairie de Honfleur, cat. n° 29
1956 Galerie Katia Granoff, Pari, cat. n° 7
1992 Musée Eugène Boudin and Grenier à Sel,
Honfleur, cat. n° 19

Bibliography
Catalogues of the Musée Eugène Boudin, 1911
(n° 14), 1959 (n° 83)
R. Schmit, 1973, vol. I, n° 162
Y. Le Pichon, *Les Peintres du Bonheur*, Paris,
1983, p. 67

---

*It is interesting to compare this work with
Monet's still-life* Side of Meat, *1864 (oil on
canvas, 24 x 33 cm., Musée d'Orsay, Paris, RF
1675), painted at a time when the two artists
were seeing each other at Honfleur and Le
Havre.*

7 CRAB, LOBSTER AND FISH, called STILL-LIFE WITH
SKATE, before 1861

Oil on canvas 72 x 97 cm.
Monogram bottom right 'E.B.'
Gift of Mme Katia Granoff, 1963 (Inv. 963-1-1)

Exhibition
1992 Musée Eugène Boudin and Grenier à Sel,
Honfleur, cat. n° 22 (ill. p. 24)

Bibliography
R. Schmit, 1973, vol. I, n° 59
L. Manœuvre, *Boudin et la Normandie*, 1991, p. 32

---

*Boudin made no mention of skate in the title of
the work, but the reference to Chardin's
painting (Musée du Louvre) was so strong that
the title ended up winning the day. Chardin
inspired many painters of still-lifes,
particularly those who, like Boudin, proved
sensitive to realism and the painting of the
Northern schools. Many variations on the
theme of skate were made in the course of the
19th century, including one by Amand Gautier,
placed on loan by the French state at the Musée
de Rochefort in 1896 (Archives de France, Fonds
F 21), and another by Adolphe-Félix Cals
(Musée Eugène Boudin). Like Chardin, Boudin
presents everyday utensils and a white dish-
cloth before a recess. Chardin, however,
introduces a humourous touch with the terrified
cat and the curious smile of the skate. At this
stage, Boudin is shown to be less preoccupied
with light than Chardin. Vente Boudin,
Le Havre, 10 January, 1861, n° 15, estimated
at 30 francs, purchased for 46 francs by Valls;
Galerie Georges Petit, Paris; Hôtel Drouot,
Paris, 16 May 1925, n° 58; Jean Schmit, Paris;
Mme Loriot, Paris; Hôtel Drouot, Paris, 27
May, 1963, n° 87, 8,500 francs.*

Still-Life with a Leg of Lamb
c. 1859

CAT. 6

Crab, Lobster and Fish, called *Still-Life with Skate,*
before 1861

Cat. 7

8 MULLET AND FISH, c. 1873

Oil on canvas, 71 x 97 cm.
Unsigned, n.d.
Eugène Boudin bequest, 1899 (Inv. 899-1-17)

Exhibition
1956 Galerie Katia Granoff, Paris, cat. n° 11
1996–1997 Bunkamura Museum of Art,
Tokyo ; Mie Prefectural Museum of Art, Tsu ;
Mito Museum of Modern Art, Ibaraki (Japan)

Bibliography
Catalogue of the Musée Eugène Boudin, 1911
(n° 11), 1959 (n° 84)

_A preparatory watercolour is preserved in the
Département des Arts Graphiques du Musée
du Louvre et du Musée d'Orsay (Still-Life
with Mullet, c. 1853, RF 16869)_

9 FISH, SKATE AND DOGFISH, c. 1873

Oil on canvas, 70 x 97 cm.
Unsigned, n.d.
Eugène Boudin bequest, 1899 (Inv. 899-1-18)

Exhibition
1956 Paris, Galerie Katia Granoff, cat. n° 12

Bibliography
Catalogues of the Musée Eugène Boudin,
1911 (n° 12), 1959 (n° 68)
R. Schmit, 1973, vol. I, n° 605

10 PHEASANT, DUCK AND FRUIT, 1879

Oil on canvas, 61 x 50 cm.
Monogram and date top right 'E.B.18 9bre 79'
Eugène Boudin bequest, 1899 (Inv. 899-1-21)

Exhibitions
1899 École Nationale des Beaux-Arts, Paris.
1956 Galerie Katia Granoff, Paris, cat. n° 17
1958 Galerie Lucien Blanc, Aix-en-Provence,
cat. n° 12
1984–1985 Sendai, Sapporo, Tokyo, Nagoya
(Japan), cat. n° 5
1985 Salon d'Automne, Galeries Nationales
du Grand Palais, Paris, cat. n° 3
1988 Museum of Modern Art, Ibaraki (Japan),
cat. n° 48 (ill. p. 92)
1996–1997 Bunkamura Museum of Art,
Tokyo; Mie Prefectural Museum of Art, Tsu ;
Mito Museum of Modern Art, Ibaraki (Japan)

Bibliography
Catalogues of the Musée Eugène Boudin,
1911 (n° 20), 1959 (n° 63)
R. Schmit, 1973, vol. II, n° 1268
L. Manœuvre, _Boudin et la Normandie_, 1991,
p. 34

Mullet and Fish
c. 1873

Fish, Skate and Dogfish

c. 1873

CAT. 9

Pheasant, Duck and Fruit
1879
CAT. 10

11 STILL-LIFE WITH FOWL (title in the exhibition catalogue of 1899, n° 308),

or STILL-LIFE WITH PHEASANT AND BASKET OF APPLES, c. 1879

Oil on canvas, 59 x 74 cm.
Signed bottom right 'E. Boudin'
Eugène Boudin bequest, 1899 (Inv. 899-1-19)

Exhibitions
1956 Galerie Katia Granoff, Paris, cat. n° 25
1988 Musée des Beaux-Arts, Caen, cat. n° 24 (ill. p. 33)
1992 Musée Eugène Boudin and Grenier à Sel, Honfleur, cat. n° 76 (ill. p. 27)

Bibliography
Catalogues of the Musée Eugène Boudin, 1911 (n° 13), 1959 (n° 78), 1983 (p. 35)
R. Schmit, 1973, vol. II, n° 1448

Another still-life, very similar in subject and technique, and likewise preserved at the Musée Eugène Boudin (cat. 10), is dated 1879, a date that can probably be adopted for the work shown here. This is one of Boudin's last still-lifes (cf. R. Schmit, 1973, where this painting is dated 1880–1885).

Still-Life with Fowl or *Still-Life with Pheasant and Basket of Apples*
c. 1879

CAT. 11

53

3 THE ESTUARY, 1845–1865

Eugène Boudin was born in Honfleur on 12 July, 1824. On 25 August that same year, an exhibition opened at the Salon in Paris that was to reveal to public and artists alike the works of the English landscape painters and the French Romantic school. Among those exhibiting at the Salon were six artists who had chosen to present landscapes inspired by Honfleur: Alexandre Colin, Louis Garneray, Xavier Leprince and his brother Léopold, Charles Renoux and François Ricois. All were classically trained artists who had succumbed to the charms of sketching landscapes after nature, a prelude to the studies that were to develop a few years later.

Honfleur already had something of a reputation at the time, and ever since the late 18th century, travellers, sketchers, lithographers and painters had been depicting the historic little town with its medieval air. Some were astonished by its appearance, others disheartened. Stendhal spoke of the ugliness of the port and confessed: 'I cannot accustom myself to this beach of mud'.[1] The town is picturesque, but the houses with their dark wooden panels are wholly lacking in comfort. The town is nevertheless enchanting, for it is protected by two high green hills, the Côte de Grâce and the Côte Vassal, whose panoramic view of the estuary and sea fired the Romantic imagination.

By 1824, Huet and Isabey were already regular visitors to the town, and their romanticism was tinged with atmospheric naturalism. Boudin was five or six years old when Corot was working at Honfleur near the Old Dock, the Calvaire de Notre-Dame-de-Grâce or at the Ferme Saint-Siméon. The two men would later meet and be bound by a deep friendship. Corot was leading the way towards a new form of painting which Boudin judged to be 'the most skilful of them all';[2] this did not stop Corot buying pastel drawings from Boudin and naming him 'The King of the Skies' for posterity.

It was in a small town frequented by artists, then, that Boudin spent his early childhood near the port and the fishing boats. Honfleur was still a busy port at the time. If deep-sea fishing was now on the way out, the northern timber industry and the export trade from the Pays d'Auge were sufficiently flourishing for plans to be made to enlarge the port and refurbish the commercial docks. These childhood visions of fishermen at work and great sailing-boats at their moorings remained engraved in the mind of Boudin, who, throughout his life, payed homage to these men who worked by the sea.

[1] Stendhal, *Mémoires d'un Touriste*, 1838.

[2] Gérard Jean-Aubry, 1968, p. 41.

In 1835, the Boudin family settled 'across the water' in Le Havre, and in 1836, at twelve years of age, Eugène started on professional life with the stationer Alphonse Lemasle. After founding his own company with Jean Acher in 1844, Boudin had an opportunity to show his early attempts at drawing to Millet, on his way through Le Havre. Millet tried in vain to dissuade the young man from taking up the artist's life, describing the difficulties which lay in store. Boudin now underwent, as Millet had warned him, his thirty days in the wilderness, returning time and again, in the reflections he confided to his notebooks, to his worries about lack of money and his dejection; at the same time, he was kept going by a ferocious will and a deep-rooted optimism that allowed him to say: 'the future is a child of the present, the sky is often blue'.[3] On 15 June, 1847, Boudin wrote that he was 'poverty stricken', but on 17 June his courage returned: 'miracle . . . two paintings sold . . . two hundred-sous pieces'.[4]

Boudin's life was spent in Normandy to either side of the Seine, close to his parents, who helped him through his poverty. In August 1849, however, he had an opportunity to travel to Belgium, where he was able to take a closer look at the works of the Flemish and Dutch painters. On his return, he received a few commissions for copies and made a number of seascapes near Le Havre. In 1850, buoyed up by the support of Alphonse Karr, Couture and Troyon, Boudin applied for a scholarship from the town of Le Havre. In February 1851, he was awarded a three-year grant, at a rate of 300 francs per quarter (roughly 5,500 francs in today's money). For Boudin this was a small fortune, part of which he left to be managed by his mother. He now divided his time between Le Havre and Honfleur in Normandy, and trips to Paris, where he trained his self-taught eye by copying paintings at the Louvre.

His constant need to return to Normandy was an expression of his uncertainty about the future and of the anguish he felt at cutting himself off from his roots. Though he knew that his friends would be there to welcome him in Paris and to offer him advice and a studio, he wasn't quite ready yet. In July 1854, Boudin moved into the Saint-Siméon Inn, but would continue paying rent in Honfleur until 1862. Between 1854 and 1859 (the year he first took part in the Salon), what kind of work was Boudin doing? Who was he seeing?

The *catalogue raisonné* of his works, his letters and private diaries, and the books written by those close to him (Gustave Cahen, Gérard Jean-Aubry) are like pieces in a gigantic

3. Gérard Jean-Aubry, unpublished notes, private collection.

4. *Ibid*.

puzzle that it's hard to put together. In 1854, his girlfriend in Honfleur, Virginie, died. For the next few years, he spent the summer painting and sketching at Saint-Siméon: the tables beneath the apple-trees, the trees of the Côte de Grâce, the cows near the estuary and the port at Honfleur.

He painted small beach-scenes with fishing boats and figures, as mentioned by his friend the Swiss painter Léon Berthoud: 'I hope to discover that you have made a great many paintings with lots of fine sailors looking out to sea'.[5] Berthoud mentions the aid provided by photography when memorising subjects: 'You'll have made the most of those lovely studies Lemarcis told me about, carried out during your stay in Honfleur; you've taken some photographs, you say, they must come in particularly handy for figure groups'.[6]

Boudin was in a good position to know about photographic techniques, since, in 1843 and 1848, two daguerreotype studios had opened in Honfleur. One was run by his friend Hamelin. The studio made portraits and 'views and landscapes', 'as they are'. Hamelin and Boudin are known to have worked together: 'I hope you've done some lovely things here in Honfleur, in company with Hamelin'.[7] In the other photographer's studio in Honfleur worked Charles-Marie Daguerre.[8] The art of photography, then, was familiar to Boudin and the painter's ally.

Throughout this period, Boudin was experimenting; he was also trying his hand at lithography, but his eyes were getting tired and he soon gave it up. In 1854, Boudin was still seeing Troyon, who was trying to help him by keeping by him in Paris small works of his that might be of interest to dealers. Had Boudin already met that master of landscape, Charles Daubigny, who had recently settled for the summer in Villerville and who painted his canvases in the open air, regardless of the weather?

Boudin still had his roots in his native Normandy, and in 1855 Berthoud teased him: 'do you know that I envy you your fate, dear friend, happy mortal who look out of your window and study the sea and the big skies. . .'.[9] It was nevertheless that same year that Boudin at last decided to change horizon and set off for Finistère in Brittany.

It was difficult for a young painter who was something of a black sheep to establish himself in Paris where support and money had to be secured. Boudin was afraid to make

5. *Ibid.*

6. *Eugène Boudin,* exhibition catalogue, Musée Eugène Boudin, Honfleur, 1992, p. 197.

7. Letter fom Léon Berthoud to Eugène Boudin, 12 October, 1854 (Gérard Jean-Aubry, unpublished notes, private collection).

8. See Charles Bréard, *Vieilles Rues, Vieilles Maisons,* Honfleur, 1900, new ed. Marseille, 1976.

9. Gérard Jean-Aubry, unpublished notes, private collection.

the move and, in 1887, explained in his recollections, that 'grey painting was hardly to anyone's taste . . . especially seascapes. [Théodore] Gudin was ensconced on the throne; Isabey went one better with natural colour. Le Poittevin and still others were all the rage, painting 'off the cuff'. . . One had to withdraw to one's province and wait for better days. . .'.[10]

Though his paintings weren't selling well, Boudin managed to find homes for a few beach-scenes and — what was new for him — in 1855 recorded in his notebooks his first sale of a still-life, a subject that would earn him a livelihood until the 1860s. Little by little, the friendships, habits and subjects that would go to make up Boudin's life were coming together. His desire for travel, of which a glimpse had been afforded in 1855, began to take shape in 1856, confirming his 'need to get this region [Honfleur, Le Havre] over with' and seek his fortune elsewhere: 'the desire to run away is tormenting me. One must try travelling, it stretches the legs'.[11] Boudin nevertheless spent part of the summer and autumn in the estuary. Henceforth, he would share his humble existence with Marie-Anne Guédès, 'la Bretonne'. From 1857 on, they would regularly spend part of the summer in Brittany, where Marie-Anne joined her family and where Boudin found numerous subjects and an authentic life. In 1857, he painted *pardons,* weddings and views of the outskirts of Quimper. 1856 and 1857 were good years, for Boudin's sales were improving. This period of relative comfort was short-lived, however, and there would still be years in which the artist's takings were meagre.

1858 – CLAUDE MONET

In 1858, Boudin wished to play a large part in the exhibition at the Société des Arts in Le Havre. He sent in eleven paintings, upholding before the town where he had grown up and that had helped him a personality that had overcome the difficult years of apprenticeship and hesitation. On 23 February, 1856, he confided in his notebook: 'I'm at last gathering some of the fruits of my ability to suffer in silence. People visit me: there are an awful lot of people, at last I'm no longer treated like an outcast. I have commissions for a little while. . . . I want to note here in passing an observation of Mathieu's, that the Romantics have had their day. I was fortunately on that path and I will persevere in it ardently. The period of my existence now coming to an end must be

10. Gérard Jean-Aubry, 1968, p. 18.

11. Journal (Musée du Louvre), quoted in *Eugène Boudin,* exhibition catalogue, Musée Eugène Boudin, Honfleur, 1992, p. 198.

decisive. I've always had a premonition of success. Will it come true? I can sense the goal at last, despite my mental torment. I can feel it: nature seen properly in all its variety and freshness, I'd be curious to see my natural sympathies coming true'.[12]

Boudin met Monet in 1858, probably in the shop where the eighteen-year-old painter was exhibiting his caricatures, and where Boudin bought his materials. As Monet remembered it, at this first meeting Boudin reproached him for compromising his talent and urged him to paint in the open air. Boudin finally persuaded the young man and dragged him off to Rouelles, a small village near Le Havre, where he explained colour to him. To Monet, Boudin's advice came like a revelation. A marvellous and fairly close friendship ensued until 1870, after which time it became more distant, though it was always present at the important moments in life such as funerals or marriages. It was in Monet's early years that Boudin's influence and advice were important. Monet later followed his own path.

THE SALON OF 1859

Boudin was thirty-four and had decided to present a large painting at the Salon, the fruit of his travels in Brittany: *The Pardon of Sainte-Anne-la-Palud.* The painting, which Baudelaire described as 'very sensible', caused no great stir and Boudin remained critical towards it, finding it 'full of defects . . . a beginner's painting'.[13]

The interest of this period lies not in Paris but in Honfleur, where Boudin met Baudelaire. Since the beginning of the year, the poet had been staying with his mother, Mme Aupick, who owned a villa known as the 'doll's house' beside the estuary near Saint-Siméon. Boudin had rented a house, said to be 'bewitched', in the rue de l'Homme de Bois, near what is now the Municipal Museum. Boudin showed Baudelaire his portfolios of pastel sketches and studies of skies, which came as a revelation to the poet. The text Baudelaire composed marked Boudin's official arrival on the artistic scene. Some of the pastels admired by Baudelaire now belong to the Musée Eugène Boudin in Honfleur: four views of Honfleur, two copies, twelves skies and six studies made at the Ferme Saint-Siméon. Boudin's small studies of cloudy blue and white skies, of moonlit night skies and stormy skies over the estuary, make up the manifesto of

12. Gérard Jean-Aubry, 1968, p. 22.

13. Notebook quoted in Gérard Jean-Aubry, 1968, p. 24.

'atmospheric' painting. They are on a par with Constable's studies of skies, the late gouaches of Isabey and the watercolours of Huet. They also look ahead to the skies of Monet who, little by little, foresook the ether to concentrate on the sea.

At the Salon of 1859, other landscape painters were exhibiting who were at the height of their fame: Louis Français presented his gigantic *Beech Trees at the Côte de Grâce,* and Charles Daubigny *Le Pré des Graves at Villerville.* These Barbizon painters had found near Honfleur an agreeable spot at which to meet and a unique light. The Ferme Saint-Siméon near the Côte de Grâce was hospitable and well-situated, and it was here that painters and artists of all backgrounds and regions would get together.

Though very little documentation concerning the establishment, either painted or printed, has survived, humorous accounts given in 1859 and 1865 conjur up the atmosphere of the place and the spirit of the painters who lodged there.[14] A text dated 15 May, 1859 describes a visit to the 'Saint-Siméon museum', which consists of various rooms in which the painters had expressed themselves on the walls by means of cartoons and landscapes (Boudin is said to have painted a 'coastal scene'), genre paintings and poems. In 1865, an article in *Le Figaro* gave a description of the farm in its leafy setting and the names of those who went there regularly. The list is not exhaustive but mentions both known and little-known names: 'Little by little, artists have learned and remembered the way there, and those whose resources keep them away from ruinously expensive hotels have come to seek a more disinterested form of hospitality at the Ferme Saint-Siméon: [Louis] Français, Matou, Stéphan Baron, [Alfred] Sainte Marie, [Jean Alexis] Achard, Jongkind, Monet, Hamelin, Amand Gautier, René Mesnard, Gustave Colin, Amédée Besnus, [Georges] Charpentier, Boyer, Courbet, mixed with men of letters: Lambert Thiboust, Alphonse Duchesne, Gustave Mathieu, Louis Pollet, Léon Reynard, Charles de Courcy and a few others of the same ilk'. These precious articles are supplemented by occasional writings and recollections by the artists themselves, amongst which, for example, *Mes Relations d'Artistes* by Amédée Besnus[15], who stayed in Honfleur many times between 1857 and 1876. In a letter written in 1896, Boudin likewise mentions the names of those who were regular visitors to the inn.[16]

These written accounts restore the works of Boudin and his friends to their rightful place in the history of landscape painting and reconstruct for us that family of artists

14. Texts published in *Honfleur avant l'Impressionnisme,* exhibition catalogue, Musée Eugène Boudin, Honfleur, July–September, 1991.
15. Paul Ollendorff, Paris, 1898.
16. Cf. p. 107.

that grew up around Honfleur — a family mistakenly known as 'The Estuary or Saint-Siméon School' and which I prefer to call 'The Gatherings at Saint-Siméon'.

JUNE 1859 – BOUDIN AND COURBET

On 16 and 17 June, 1859, Courbet met Boudin in Le Havre and followed him on to Honfleur. In what was a crucial period for Boudin, the interest shown by a major and highly regarded painter was reassuring. Few people painted as well as he did, Courbet assured him. A firm friendship was established between these two very different men, and they went a bit of the way together, with Courbet returning to the coast at Trouville and Deauville between 1864 and 1866. Like Corot before him, Courbet admired Boudin's skies and confessed: 'you're a seraph . . . you're the only one who knows about the sky'. In certain works that Courbet made around this time, a shift may be discerned in his treatment of skies and beaches, influenced perhaps by the breadth with which they are rendered in Boudin's seaside scenes and seascapes.

Up until 1862, Boudin spent several months of each year at his home in Honfleur. We have seen how hesitant he was to leave the province, how difficult he found it to come to terms with life in Paris. In 1862, he asked his friend Gustave Mathieu for advice: 'This year I'd once again resolved to go to Paris and try to get along there as best I could, with the aid of a few people, foremost amongst whom I put you; but the accounts I'm given of the state of affairs in Paris frighten me, all the more so as I don't have any advances and, in order to live, would have to find homes — all too hypothetical, alas! — for my paintings.
No-one is better placed than you to know the true state of affairs; tell me quite sincerely what you think. You see painters and art-lovers and can tell me how things really stand.
I confess that I can no longer find enough to live on here — literally; one has to find a living somewhere'.[17]
He gradually decides to settle in the capital, for 'Paris, this devil of a city, is really the only place where you can develop your faculties. There's an example at every step, and people who goad you into moving forward. . .'.[18]

17. Gustave Cahen, 1900, pp. 39–40.
18. Gérard Jean-Aubry, 1968, p. 54.

Boudin needed to be goaded and believed in the virtues of exchange. Though a 'lonely' figure and an independent spirit, he was an honest and attentive man, and highly self-critical: 'I'm going to take another look at what the others are up to, out of curiosity and also to profit from whatever's good about them: perfection is collective work. . . '.[19]

After years of remaining loyal to the estuary, Boudin, now settled in Paris, would return home regularly to drink in the atmosphere of his youth, renting a house each summer in Trouville. Boudin's Honfleur works date mainly from the years 1845 to 1869. Some 120 paintings and a great many drawings describe the landscapes of Honfleur, the Côte de Grâce, the pasture-land bordering the estuary, the Saint-Siméon Inn, the port and the banks of the Seine from Vasouy to Le Poudreux. After 1869, the Honfleur paintings become more scarce, the last of these being painted between 1880 and 1897. To these Honfleur works must be added the studies he made at Sainte Adresse and Le Havre. Boudin's loyalty to the region of his childhood is obvious. It was kept alive by friends, such as Dubourg and Hamelin, who had remained in Honfleur, and by his family in Le Havre, foremost among whom his brother, Louis, with whom he corresponded. The good years were many: 1859 with Courbet and Baudelaire, 1863 and 1865 with Jongkind, and from 1864 to 1870 with Bazille and Monet.

Whenever Boudin seemed to be growing distant from Honfleur, projects would bring him back — in 1868, when Dubourg created the Municipal Museum; and in 1896 — by which time Boudin was a well-known figure — when the ethnographic society 'Le Vieux Honfleur' was clamouring for him to sit on its committee. In 1897, Boudin, who was already ill by this time, may have sensed that he was making his final voyage. He wanted to do 'a few studies in Honfleur, the market, the port'.

The works owned by the Musée Eugène Boudin relating to Honfleur and the estuary concern the period 1845 to 1865: pencil studies of fishermen and seaside scenes, skies above the estuary, studies at Saint-Siméon and a view of the Trouville road. A few later paintings (c. 1880) recall Boudin's repeated homecomings during the last twenty years of his life. The works he bequeathed to the museum reflect his love of his native town and the interest he took in setting up a museum designed 'to give the people of Honfleur a taste for the Fine Arts' and to perpetuate the memory of those artists, his friends, who frequented Honfleur throughout the 19th century.

19. *Ibid.*, p. 42.

12 THE MOULIN DU PERREY AT LE HAVRE, 1848

Charcoal drawing with highlights of coloured
pastels on blue-grey paper pasted onto paper
and board, 30.1 x 46.8 cm.
Signed and dated bottom right
'E. Boudin. 1848', superimposed stamp
bottom left, figure '6' underlined
Hambourg-Rachet donation, 1988
(Inv. 988-1-9)

Exhibition
1992 Musée Eugène Boudin and Grenier à Sel,
Honfleur, cat. n° 178

Bibliography
*Donation Hambourg-Rachet au Musée Eugène
Boudin*, 1988, cat. n° 9, p. 22
L. Manœuvre, *Eugène Boudin, Dessins*, 1991,
p. 157

13 THE SHIPWRECK, c. 1848

Charcoal drawing with highlights of white
chalk on beige paper pasted onto paper and
board, 25.2 x 36.1 cm.
Stamped bottom right 'E.B.'
Hambourg-Rachet donation, 1988
(Inv. 988-1-10)

Exhibitions
1958 Galerie Charpentier, Paris
1992 Musée Eugène Boudin and Grenier à Sel,
Honfleur, cat. n° 182

Bibliography
*Donation Hambourg-Rachet au Musée Eugène
Boudin*, 1988, cat. n° 10, p. 23
L. Manœuvre, *Eugène Boudin, Dessins*, 1991,
p. 89

*This early drawing still shows traces of
Isabey's seascapes and shipwrecks,
suggesting a certain line of descent between
Isabey and the generation of Boudin and
Jongkind. Isabey had been walking in
Normandy since 1820 and had worked at
Honfleur in 1826 (one of his views of the
beach at Honfleur was presented at the Salon
of 1827), 1854, 1858, 1859, 1866, etc. He
met Boudin at Le Havre in 1845 and gave
him a number of tips.*

The Moulin du Perrey at Le Havre
1848

Cat. 12

The Shipwreck
c. 1848

CAT. 13

14 PORTRAIT OF THE ARTIST'S FATHER, c. 1850

Oil on paper mounted on board backed on oak,
29.2 x 22.5 cm.
Unsigned, n.d.
Eugène Boudin bequest, 1899 (Inv. 899-1-1)

Exhibitions
1953 Mairie de Honfleur, cat. n° 27
1956 Galerie Katia Granoff, Paris, cat. n° 1
1992 Musée Eugène Boudin and Grenier à Sel,
Honfleur, cat. n° 10. (ill. p. 173)

Bibliography
Catalogues of the Musée Eugène Boudin, 1911
(n° 10), 1959 (n° 70)
R. L. Benjamin, *Eugène Boudin*, Paris, 1937 (ill p. 180)
R. Schmit, 1973, vol. I, n° 6

*Laurent Manœuvre dates this c. 1855–1860
(see* Eugène Boudin, *exhibition catalogue, 1992).
Gilbert de Knyff dates it c.1853–1854 (see G. de
Knyff, 1976, p. 44). This portrait was found on the
back of a beach scene (cat. 77). The two works
were separated in 1954. Léonard-Sébastien Boudin
(1789–1863), the artist's father, is thought to have
been a Newfoundland fisherman. He settled in Le
Havre in 1825, where he worked on the boats
operating between Le Havre and Hamburg (see
Gérard Jean-Aubry, 1968). From 1838 to 1862, he
was a seaman on 'Le Français', a steamship
operating between Le Havre and Honfleur. This
magnificent sketch is imbued with the studies
Boudin had made of the Flemish painters. The light
is concentrated in the face, the rest of the body being
conjured up by large brush-strokes.*

Portrait of the Artist's Father
c. 1850
CAT. 14

Sailing Ships and Boats
outside Honfleur
c. 1854–1860

Cat. 15

Boats outside Honfleur
c. 1854–1860

Cat. 16

Boats and Fishermen
c. 1854–1860

CAT. 17

Boats on the Shore,
c. 1854–1860

CAT. 18

15 SAILING SHIPS AND BOATS OUTSIDE HONFLEUR, c. 1854–1860

Pencil drawing on beige paper, 9 x 13.8 cm.
Gift of Dr. Georges Bréhier, 1966
(Inv. 966-2-1)

16 BOATS OUTSIDE HONFLEUR, c. 1854–1860

Pencil drawing on beige paper, 9 x 12.5 cm.
Illegible annotations bottom left
Inscribed on the back in pencil *'Bateaux de
fond nombreux et peu perceptibles sur mer vert
d'eau... de ces reflets plus clairs qui la
distinguent du ciel — longues voiles brunes
sombres... massif'* [partly illegible]
Gift of Dr. Georges Bréhier, 1966
(Inv. 966-2-2)

17 BOATS AND FISHERMEN, c. 1854–1860

Pencil drawing on greyish-brown paper,
14.5 x 21 cm.
Pencil annotations, inscribed in ink top right
'Cent cinquante neuf' and '880'
Marest-Devillers bequest, 1979 (Inv. 980-1-1)

18 BOATS ON THE SHORE, c. 1854–1860

Graphite and pencil drawing on beige paper
pasted onto paper and board, 13.2 x 21.4 cm.
Stamped bottom right 'E.B.', graphite pencil
annotations *'profond, vert fin, bl[anc/bleu?], vert
jaune'*
Hambourg-Rachet donation, 1988
(Inv. 988-1-16)

Exhibition
1992 Musée Eugène Boudin and Grenier à Sel,
Honfleur, cat. n° 214

Bibliography
*Donation Hambourg-Rachet au Musée Eugène
Boudin*, 1988, cat. n° 16, p. 32

*Women and Men
next to a Boat,*
c. 1854–1860

*Groups near Beached
Boats,*
c. 1854–1860

19 WOMEN AND MEN NEXT TO A BOAT,
c. 1854–1860

Graphite and pencil drawing on beige paper
pasted onto paper and board, 12.9 x 20.8 cm.
Stamped bottom right 'E.B', graphite pencil
annotations *'violet, bleu, rose, jaune, ch[aud¿],
plate grande'*
Hambourg-Rachet donation, 1988
(Inv. 988-1-14)

Exhibition
1992 Musée Eugène Boudin and Grenier à Sel,
Honfleur, cat. n° 196

Bibliography
*Donation Hambourg-Rachet au Musée Eugène
Boudin, 1988, cat. n° 14, p. 25*

20 GROUPS NEAR BEACHED BOATS,
c. 1854–1860

Graphite and pencil drawing on beige paper
pasted onto paper and board, 11.2 x 16.4 cm.
Stamped bottom right 'E.B.', graphite pencil
annotations on the 'blue' sky
Hambourg-Rachet donation, 1988
(Inv. 988-1-15)

Bibliography
*Donation Hambourg-Rachet au Musée Eugène
Boudin, 1988, cat. n° 15, p. 32*

21 THREE FISHERMEN ON THE JETTY,
c. 1854–1860

Pencil and graphite drawing on beige paper
pasted onto paper and board, 11 x 12.5 cm.
Stamped bottom right 'E.B.', graphite pencil
annotation *'jaunâtre'* [¿]
Hambourg-Rachet donation, 1988
(Inv. 988-1-11)

Exhibition
1992 Musée Eugène Boudin and Grenier à Sel,
Honfleur, cat. n° 201

Bibliography
*Donation Hambourg-Rachet au Musée Eugène
Boudin, 1988, cat. n° 11, p. 24*

Three Fishermen on the Jetty
c. 1854–1860

CAT. 21

22 FISHERMAN WEARING A BONNET,
c. 1854–1860

Pencil drawing on beige paper pasted onto
paper and board, 19.5 x 12.2 cm.
Stamped bottom right 'E.B', graphite pencil
annotations *'rouge vif, jaune clair, rougeâtre'*
Hambourg-Rachet donation, 1988
(Inv. 988-1-12)

Exhibition
1992 Musée Eugène Boudin and Grenier à Sel,
Honfleur, cat. n° 202

Bibliography
*Donation Hambourg-Rachet au Musée Eugène
Boudin*, 1988, cat. n° 12, p. 24

23 FISHERMAN LOOKING THROUGH A TELESCOPE,
c. 1854–1860

Pencil drawing on beige paper pasted onto
paper and board, 12 x 16.2 cm.
Stamped bottom right 'E.B.'
Hambourg-Rachet donation, 1988
(Inv. 988-1-13)

Exhibition
1992 Musée Eugène Boudin and Grenier à Sel,
Honfleur, cat. n° 198

Bibliography
*Donation Hambourg-Rachet au Musée Eugène
Boudin*, 1988, cat. n° 13, p. 25

Fisherman Wearing a Bonnet
c. 1854–1860

CAT. 22

Fisherman Looking through a Telescope
c. 1854–1860

CAT. 23

Skies

Aesthetic Curios

Yes, imagination makes the landscape. I understand that a spirit set on taking notes cannot abandon itself to the prodigious reveries contained in the spectacles presented by nature: but why does the imagination flee the landscape painter's studio? Perhaps artists who cultivate the genre are far too wary of their memory and adopt a method of immediate copying that is perfectly adapted to their idle minds. If they had seen, as I did recently at the home of M. Boudin — who, be it said in passing, has exhibited a very good and very sensible painting (*The Pardon of Sainte-Anne-la-Palud*) — several hundred pastel studies, improvised facing sea and sky, they would understand what they do not appear to understand, namely the difference that separates a study from a painting. But M. Boudin, who might pride himself on his devotion to his art, shows his curious collection with great modesty. He knows full well that it must all become a painting, by means of the poetic impression recalled at will: and he does not pretend to pass his notes off for paintings. Later, without any doubt, he will display for us in his finished paintings the wondrous magics of air and water. These studies, so swiftly and accurately sketched, after what, in terms of force and colour, are the most inconstant, the most fleeting of things, after waves and clouds, always have written in their margins the date, the hour and the wind: thus, for example, 8 October, noon, wind from the north-west. If you have occasionally had leisure to acquaint yourself with these meteorological beauties, you could verify from memory the exactitude of M. Boudin's observations. Hiding the caption with your hand, you would guess the season, the hour and the wind. I exaggerate nothing. I have seen. At the end, all these clouds with their fantastic, luminous shapes, these chaotic shadows, these green and pink immensities suspended and added one on top of the other, these yawning ovens, these firmaments made from black or violet satin, crumpled, rolled or torn, these horizons in mourning or streaming with molten metal, all these depths, all these splendours, went to my head like an intoxicating drink or the eloquence of opium. It is rather curious, not once faced with all this liquid or aerial magic did I complain about the absence of man. But I will certainly refrain from drawing from the fullness of my delight advice for anyone, any more than for M. Boudin. The advice would be too dangerous. Let him remember that man, as Robespierre, who had received a sound classical education, once said, never sees man without pleasure: and if he wants to win a little popularity, let him certainly refrain from thinking the public has reached an equal enthusiasm for solitude.

Charles Baudelaire, 'Salon of 1859', VII, Landscape

Fine Weather on the Estuary
c. 1854–1859

24 FINE WEATHER ON THE ESTUARY,
c. 1854–1859

Pastel on blue-grey paper, 16 x 21 cm.
Monogram bottom right 'E.B.'
Eugène Boudin bequest 1899 (Inv. 899-1-34)

Exhibitions
1899 École Nationale des Beaux-Arts, Paris.
1956 Galerie Katia Granoff, Paris, cat. n° 37
1992 Musée Eugène Boudin and Grenier à Sel,
Honfleur, cat. n° 234

Bibliography
Catalogues of the Musée Eugène Boudin,
1911 (n° 171), 1959 (n° 30)

_____

This drawing may be unfinished.

25 WHITE CLOUDS OVER THE ESTUARY,
c. 1854–1859

Pastel on blue-grey paper, 14.7 x 21 cm.
Monogram bottom right 'E.B.'
Eugène Boudin bequest, 1899 (Inv. 899-1-37)

Exhibitions
1899 École Nationale des Beaux-Arts, Paris
1956 Galerie Katia Granoff, Paris, cat. n° 41
1992 Musée Eugène Boudin and Grenier à Sel,
Honfleur, cat. n° 238

Bibliography
Catalogues of the Musée Eugène Boudin, 1911
(n° 171), 1959 (n° 28), 1983 (p. 40)
J. Isaacson, *Observation and Reflection. Claude
Monet*, New York, 1978, fig. 6, p. 27
F. Arcangeli, *Monet*, Bologna, 1989, fig. 7
L. Manœuvre, *Eugène Boudin, Dessins,* 1991, p. 22
L. Manœuvre, 1994, p. 10

White Clouds over the Estuary
c. 1854–1859

Tuesday, 3 December, 1856.

To swim in the open sky. To achieve a cloud's *tenderness*. To suspend those background masses, far of in the grey mist, and break up the azure. I feel it all coming, dawning in my intentions. What delight and what torment! If the bottom was still, perhaps I would never achieve those depths. Did they do better in the past? Did the Dutchmen achieve that poetry of clouds I seek? That tenderness of the sky which even extends to admiration, to worship: it's no exaggeration.

Unpublished notebook, quoted
in Gérard Jean-Aubry, *Eugène Boudin,* p. 22

Boudin's portfolio and easel

CAT. XI and XII

White Clouds, Blue Sky
c. 1859

<small>CAT. 26</small>

26 WHITE CLOUDS, BLUE SKY, c. 1859

Pastel on blue-grey paper, 148 x 210 cm.
Monogram bottom right 'E.B.'
Eugène Boudin bequest, 1899 (Inv. 899-1-36)

Exhibitions
1899 École Nationale des Beaux-Arts, Paris
1956 Galerie Katia Granoff, Paris, cat. n° 40
1992 Musée Eugène Boudin and Grenier à Sel,
Honfleur, cat. n° 237

Bibliography
Catalogues of the Musée Eugène Boudin,
1911 (n° 171), 1959 (n° 59), 1993 (p. 57)
Y. Le Pichon, *Les Peintres du Bonheur,* Paris,
1983, cat. n° 57.1, p. 56

27 WHITE CLOUDS, c. 1854–1859

Pastel on blue-grey paper, 16.1 x 21 cm.
Monogram bottom right 'E.B.'
Eugène Boudin bequest, 1899 (Inv. 899-1-35)

Exhibitions
1899 École Nationale des Beaux-Arts, Paris
1956 Galerie Katia Granoff, Paris, cat. n° 39
1992 Musée Eugène Boudin and Grenier à Sel,
Honfleur, cat. n° 239 (ill. p. 55)

Bibliography
Catalogues of the Musée Eugène Boudin,
1911 (n° 171), 1959 (n° 26), 1983 (cover)
Videodisk, The Museum Education
Consortium, New York, 1990

28 FINE WEATHER, WHITE CLOUDS, c. 1859

Pastel on blue-grey paper, 15 x 21.8 cm.
Monogram bottom right 'E.B.'
Eugène Boudin bequest, 1899 (Inv. 899-1-33)

Exhibitions
1899 École Nationale des Beaux-Arts, Paris
1956 Galerie Katia Granoff, Paris, cat. n° 38
1992 Musée Eugène Boudin and Grenier à Sel,
Honfleur, cat. n° 235

Bibliography
Catalogues of the Musée Eugène Boudin,
1911 (n° 171), 1959 (n° 32)

29 BLUE SKY, WHITE CLOUDS, c. 1854–1859

Pastel on blue-grey paper, 16.2 x 21 cm.
Monogram bottom right 'E.B.'
Eugène Boudin bequest, 1899 (Inv. 899-1-32)

Exhibitions
1899 École Nationale des Beaux-Arts, Paris
1956 Galerie Katia Granoff, Paris, cat. n° 36
1992 Musée Eugène Boudin and Grenier à Sel,
Honfleur, cat. n° 236

Bibliography
Catalogues of the Musée Eugène Boudin,
1911 (n° 171), 1959 (n° 34)
L. Manœuvre, *Eugène Boudin, Dessins,* 1991,
p. 23
Videodisk, Musées de Basse-Normandie, 1994

White Clouds
c. 1854–1859

Fine Weather, White Clouds
c. 1859

Blue Sky, White Clouds
c. 1854–1859

<small>CAT. 29</small>

Boat in the Estuary
c. 1854–1860

Cat. 30

Boat at Low Tide, Outside of Honfleur
c. 1854–1860

<small>Cat. 31</small>

30 Boat in the estuary, c. 1854–1860

Pastel on paper, 14.6 x 21 cm.
Signed bottom left 'E. Boudin', double
stamped bottom right
Gift of Georges Sporck, 1934 (Inv. 934-1-3)

Exhibition
1992 Musée Eugène Boudin and Grenier à Sel,
Honfleur, cat. n° 228

Bibliography
Catalogues of the Musée Eugène Boudin,
1959 (n° 33)

31 Boat at low tide, outside HONFLEUR, c. 1854–1860

Pastel on paper, 15.4 x 20.8 cm.
Signed bottom left 'E. Boudin'
Gift of Georges Sporck, 1934
(Inv. 934-1-2)

Exhibition
1992 Musée Eugène Boudin and Grenier à Sel,
Honfleur, cat. n° 227

Bibliography
Catalogues of the Musée Eugène Boudin,
1959 (n° 29)
L. Manœuvre, *Eugène Boudin, Dessins,* 1991,
p. 88 (n° 98)

*G*ift of the composer Georges Sporck to the

*museum in 1934. His father, Jules Sporck,
was a friend of Boudin and Corot. Boudin
dedicated a painting of 1896,* The Return of
the Fishing Boats at Trouville *(private
collection, Schmit 3578)* 'À son petit ami
Georges Sporck'.

32 Sunset and cliff (Etretat), c. 1854–1859

Pastel on blue-grey paper, 15 x 20.8 cm.
Monogram bottom right 'E.B.', illegible
annotations ['. . . *voilé'*] near lower edge,
partly concealed by the pastel
Eugène Boudin bequest, 1899 (Inv. 899-1-42)

Exhibitions
1899 École Nationale des Beaux-Arts, Paris
1956 Galerie Katia Granoff, Paris, cat. n° 42.5
1957 Bibliothèque Nationale, Paris,
cat. n° 361
1992 Musée Eugène Boudin and Grenier à Sel,
Honfleur, cat. n° 242 (ill. p. 56)

Bibliography:
Catalogues of the Musée Eugène Boudin,
1911 (n° 172), 1959 (n° 39), 1993 (p. 56)
L. Manœuvre, *Eugène Boudin, Dessins,* 1991,
p. 28
Videodisk, Musées de Basse-Normandie, 1994

Sunset and Cliff (Etretat)
c. 1854–1859

<small>Cat. 32</small>

33 OVERCAST SKY AT SEA, c. 1854–1859

Pastel on blue-grey paper, 15 x 20.3 cm.
Monogram bottom right 'E.B.', illegible
annotations near lower edge
Eugène Boudin bequest, 1899 (Inv. 899-1-43)

Exhibitions
1899 École Nationale des Beaux-Arts, Paris
1956 Galerie Katia Granoff, Paris, cat. n° 42.6
1957 Bibliothèque Nationale, Paris, cat. n° 361
1992 Musée Eugène Boudin and Grenier à Sel,
Honfleur, cat. n° 240 (ill. p. 58)

Bibliography
Catalogues of the Musée Eugène Boudin,
1911 (n° 172), 1959 (n° 39)
L. Manœuvre, *Eugène Boudin, Dessins,* 1991,
p. 29

34 THE MOON RISING OVER THE ESTUARY,
c. 1854–1859

Pastel on paper, 14 x 21.1 cm.
Monogram bottom right 'E.B.'
Eugène Boudin bequest, 1899 (Inv. 899-1-40)

Exhibitions
1899 École Nationale des Beaux-Arts, Paris
1956 Galerie Katia Granoff, Paris, cat. n° 42.3
1957 Bibliothèque Nationale, Paris,
cat. n° 361
1992 Musée Eugène Boudin and Grenier à Sel,
Honfleur, cat. n° 243

Bibliography
Catalogues of the Musée Eugène Boudin,
1911 (n° 172), 1959 (n° 39)
L. Manœuvre, *Eugène Boudin, Dessins,* 1991,
p. 30

35 SUNSET AT SEA, c. 1854–1859

Pastel on blue-grey paper, 14.1 x 21.1 cm.
Monogram bottom right 'E.B.'
Eugène Boudin bequest, 1899 (Inv. 899-1-41)

Exhibitions
1899 École Nationale des Beaux-Arts, Paris
1956 Galerie Katia Granoff, Paris, cat. n° 42.4
1957 Bibliothèque Nationale, Paris, cat. n° 361
1992 Musée Eugène Boudin and Grenier à Sel,
Honfleur, cat. n° 241, ill. p. 62

Bibliography
Catalogues of the Musée Eugène Boudin,
1911 (n° 172), 1959 (n° 39)
L. Manœuvre, *Eugène Boudin, Dessins,* 1991,
p. 30

Overcast Sky at Sea
c. 1854–1859

The Moon Rising over the Estuary
c. 1854–1859

Sunset at Sea
c. 1854–1859

Cat. 35

36 CLOUDY SKY AND MOON, c. 1854–1859

Pastel on blue-grey paper, 13.8 x 18.8 cm.
Monogram bottom right 'E.B.'
Eugène Boudin bequest, 1899 (Inv. 899-1-38)

Exhibitions
1899 École Nationale des Beaux-Arts, Paris
1956 Galerie Katia Granoff, Paris, cat. n° 42.1
1957 Bibliothèque Nationale, Paris, cat. n° 361
1992 Musée Eugène Boudin and Grenier à Sel,
Honfleur, cat. n° 244 (ill. p. 59)

Bibliography
Catalogues of the Musée Eugène Boudin, 1911
(n° 172), 1959 (n° 39)
L. Manœuvre, *Eugène Boudin, Dessins,* 1991, p. 31

On the back is a small pencil study, Sailing
Ships and Boats outside Honfleur (cat. 15).

37 MOON AND OVERCAST SKY, c. 1854–1859

Pastel on paper, 14.5 x 21.3 cm.
Monogram bottom right 'E.B.'
Eugène Boudin bequest, 1899 (Inv. 899-1-39)

Exhibitions
1899 École Nationale des Beaux-Arts, Paris
1956 Galerie Katia Granoff, Paris, cat. n° 42.2
1957 Bibliothèque Nationale, Paris,
cat. n° 361
1992 Musée Eugène Boudin and Grenier à Sel,
Honfleur, cat. n° 245 (ill. p. 63)

Bibliography
Catalogues of the Musée Eugène Boudin,
1911 (n° 172), 1959 (n° 39)
L. Manœuvre, *Eugène Boudin, Dessins,* 1991,
p. 31

Cloudy Sky and Moon
c. 1854–1859

Moon and Overcast Sky
c. 1854–1859

CAT. 37

Honfleur

38 OLD COURTYARD IN HONFLEUR, c. 1854–1959

Pastel on bluish-grey paper, 21.6 x 28.8 cm.
Unsigned
Eugène Boudin bequest, 1899 (Inv. 899-1-30)

Exhibitions
1899 École Nationale des Beaux-Arts, Paris
1952 Mairie de Honfleur
1956 Galerie Katia Granoff, Paris, cat. n° 34
1992 Musée Eugène Boudin and Grenier à Sel,
Honfleur, cat. n° 233

Bibliography
Catalogues of the Musée Eugène Boudin,
1911 (n° 169-3), 1959 (n° 40)
L. Manœuvre, *Eugène Boudin, Dessins*, 1991,
p. 114

39 PLACE SAINTE-CATHERINE AT HONFLEUR,
c. 1854–1859

Pastel on bluish-grey paper, 21.2 x 31 cm.
Unsigned
Eugène Boudin bequest, 1899 (Inv. 899-1-29)

Exhibitions
1899 École Nationale des Beaux-Arts, Paris
1952 Mairie de Honfleur
1956 Galerie Katia Granoff, Paris, cat. n° 33
1992 Musée Eugène Boudin and Grenier à Sel,
Honfleur, cat. n° 232 (ill. p. 42)

Bibliography
Catalogues of the Musée Eugène Boudin, 1911
(n° 169-4), 1959 (n° 35)
L. Manœuvre, *Eugène Boudin, Dessins*, 1991,
p. 115
Videodisk, Musées de Basse-Normandie, 1994

*The place Sainte-Catherine, with its church
and steeple, was frequently painted by artists
from the early 19th century on (Huet, Jean-
Joseph Bellel, Dubourg, Jongkind, Monet,
Dufy). As the market was held there (it is still
held there today), it attracted artists for its
picturesque qualities, while the isolated
position of the steeple astonished them. Several
drawings by Boudin representing the market
with the steeple behind are preserved in the
Département des Arts Graphiques du Musée
du Louvre et du Musée d'Orsay.*

Old Courtyard in Honfleur
c. 1854–1959

Place Sainte-Catherine at Honfleur
c. 1854–1859

CAT. 39

40 THE SMALL FISHMARKET AT HONFLEUR,
c. 1854–1859

Pastel on bluish-grey paper, 21.4 x 31.9 cm.
Unsigned
Eugène Boudin bequest, 1899 (Inv. 899-1-31)

Exhibitions
1899 École Nationale des Beaux-Arts, Paris
1952 Mairie de Honfleur
1956 Galerie Katia Granoff, Paris, cat. n° 35
1992 Musée Eugène Boudin and Grenier à Sel,
Honfleur, cat. n° 230

Bibliography
Catalogues of the Musée Eugène Boudin, 1911
(n° 69-2, ill. p. 32 bis), 1959 (n° 27)
J. Hackforth Jones, *À Table avec les
Impressionnistes*, 1991, p. 95
P. Lurie, *Guide to the Impressionist Landscape*,
Seattle, 1990
L. Manœuvre, *Eugène Boudin, Dessins*, 1991,
p. 65

*This fishmarket was situated on the south side
of the Old Dock at Honfleur (cf. cat. 41).
Boudin often took up the same themes in
Honfleur. In the 1850s and 1860s, he chose
subjects in the town, the port and the Saint-
Siméon Inn, and in 1897 made a final trip to
Honfleur as a last farewell. On 30 September,
1897, he wrote to his brother Louis: 'I'm
making a few studies in Honfleur, the market,
the port, but the shipping has fallen off here,
as it has everywhere'.*

41 THE SMALL FISHMARKET AT HONFLEUR,
c. 1854–1859

Pastel on bluish-grey paper, 22 x 30 cm.
Unsigned
Eugène Boudin bequest, 1899 (Inv. 899-1-28)

Exhibitions
1899 École Nationale des Beaux-Arts, Paris
1952 Mairie de Honfleur
1956 Galerie Katia Granoff, Paris, cat. n° 32
1992 Musée Eugène Boudin and Grenier à Sel,
Honfleur, cat. n° 229 (ill. p. 41)

Bibliography
Catalogues of the Musée Eugène Boudin,
1911 (n° 169-1), 1959 (n° 31), 1983 (p. 36),
1993 (p. 55)
L. Manœuvre, *Eugène Boudin, Dessins,* 1991,
p. 56

*This pastel drawing represents the same spot
viewed from a different angle, near what is
now the rue de la République. Boudin also
made drawings of the other fishmarket in
Honfleur, in the rue de la Ville, at the centre of
the former enclosure (see cat. 42).*

The Small Fishmarket at Honfleur
c. 1854–1859

Cat. 40

The Small Fishmarket at Honfleur
c. 1854–1859

<small>CAT. 41</small>

Fishmarket, rue de la Ville, Honfleur
c. 1854–1859

<small>Cat. 42</small>

42 FISHMARKET, RUE DE LA VILLE, HONFLEUR,
c. 1854–1859

Pastel on grey paper pasted onto paper and
board, 21.2 x 30.6 cm.
Stamped bottom right 'E.B.'
Hambourg-Rachet donation, 1988
(Inv. 988-1-2)

Exhibition
1992 Musée Eugène Boudin and Grenier à Sel,
Honfleur, cat. n° 231

Bibliography
*Donation Hambourg-Rachet au Musée Eugène
Boudin*, 1988, cat. n° 2 (ill. p. 35)
L. Manœuvre, *Eugène Boudin, Dessins,* 1991, p. 64

43 FISHMARKET, TROUVILLE (¿), c. 1875–1880

Watercolour over graphite pencil sketch with
highlights of white gouache on bluish paper,
pasted onto paper and board, 13.1 x 14.4 cm.
Stamped 'E.B.' bottom left
Hambourg-Rachet donation, 1988
(Inv. 988-1-7)

Exhibition
1992 Musée Eugène Boudin and Grenier à Sel,
Honfleur, cat. n° 312

Bibliography
*Donation Hambourg-Rachet au Musée Eugène
Boudin*, 1988, cat. n° 7 (ill. p. 30)
L. Manœuvre, *Eugène Boudin, Dessins,* 1991, p. 58

Fishmarket, Trouville (¿)
c. 1875–1880
CAT. 43

The Saint-Siméon Inn

44 THE COTTAGE IN THE COURTYARD, FERME SAINT-SIMÉON, HONFLEUR, c. 1855–1860

Oil on mahogany panel, 23.4 x 30.1 cm.
Inscribed on the back *'peinture de E. Boudin provenant de la famille de Boudin. Henri de St Delis'*
Hambourg-Rachet donation, 1988 (Inv. 988-1-1)

Bibliography
Catalogue *Donation Hambourg-Rachet au Musée Eugène Boudin*, 1988, cat. n° 1 (ill. p. 35)

45 TWILIGHT AT THE SAINT-SIMÉON INN, 1857

Oil on oak panel, 21.2 x 27.5 cm.
Unsigned, n.d.
Gift of Louis-Alexandre Dubourg, 1892
(Inv. 892-2-1)

Exhibition
1956 Galerie Katia Granoff, Paris, cat. n° 2

Bibliography
Catalogue of the Musée Eugène Boudin, 1911 (n° 9)
R. L. Benjamin, *Eugène Boudin*, 1937, ill. p. 180
R. Schmit, 1973, vol. II, n° 109

Gift of Louis-Alexandre Dubourg, founder of the Municipal Museum in 1868.

The Cottage in the Courtyard, Ferme Saint-Siméon, Honfleur
c. 1855–1860

CAT. 44

Twilight at the Saint-Siméon Inn
1857

CAT. 45

46 Two letters from Eugène Boudin,
dated 3 August and 25 October, 1896

Letter of 3 August, 1896, sent from Deauville,
four folded pages, 13.4 x 10.8 cm., brown ink
on beige paper (not reproduced here)
Letter of 25 October, 1896, sent from
Deauville, four and a half pages,
17.7 x 11.4 cm., brown ink on beige paper
Gift of Mme Guyot, 1977 (Inv. 977-5-1
and 977-5-2)

*Letters addressed to Jehan Soudan
de Pierrefitte. This letter, dated 25 October,
1896, was published by Jehan Soudan
in his newspaper* Le Petit Normand,
*8 July, 1900. Jehan Soudan falsified part
of the contents to put himself in a good
light. The letter was published in full
by Solange Lemaire in* Bulletin de la Société
des Amis du Musée Eugène Boudin,
1975–1977.

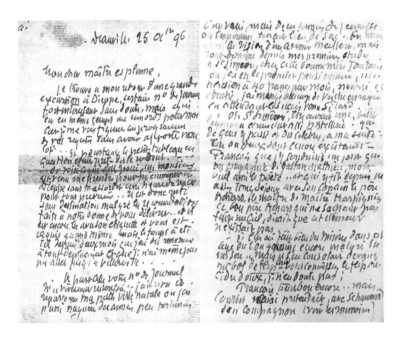

*Letter dated 25 October, 1896,
called the 'Saint-Siméon letter'*

Cat. 46

Deauville, 25 October 96

My dear *Maître ès plume,*

I find on my return from a long outing to Dieppe a particular issue of a journal, of great interest no doubt, but at the same time a cause of remorse to me, for I see myself listed on the programme for your regattas without having contributed my share. . . .
And yet the little painting in question was ready — by 20 August.
So here's what happened, a gentleman came to fetch me to take me to Dieppe without granting me an hour's respite to warn you. [The painting] thus remained without destination, despite instructions given to our maid to deliver it to you. . . . and it's still here with its label and is yours just the same, but what with the weather these last two months I've had to give up any idea of moving about and haven't even been able to get to Villerville. . . .
Apart from that, the issue of your journal interested me deeply. I saw and visited my little native town again, and though it's true I didn't have much money during the years I spent there, they were years of youth in which hope took the place of luggage.
We had a vision of a brighter future at the time, but all the same, since my first studies at St Siméon at the home of that dear Mère Toutain, where I was the first lodger . . . board and lodging at 40 francs a month, bedded and fed, I went through hard times waiting for success, which came so late.
Oh Saint-Siméon, a wonderful legend could be written about that hostelry! The number of people who came by, and famous ones, after me.
One or two of them still exist. Français, who I drove there one day who [sic] with Gustave Mathieu, my old friend the poet . . . who's since made quite a lengthy stay there with his chum, the Père Achard, Harpignies' master, dear Père Achard who, not knowing how to do a sky, said no such element existed. I gave him a very hard time at an age when you still make mischief despite the poverty, but he would console himself with a bowl of flip (hic), you know all about *flip* or sweet cider, I'm sure!

Français is still holding up. . . . But Courbet, who maintained with Schaunard his companion (see his memoirs) that the cider was only fit for washing one's hands in, fell asleep after a copious lunch washed down with Père Toutain's little barrel.
On yet another day, I took Troyon and Van Marck there, who lunched on cider. They're dead, the master sadly and prematurely. . . . The pupil had time to bring in the harvest.
I played some good games of skittles there with Diaz, another good man who knew how to throw the ball with an energetic arm and would knock the skittles down in a trice for you. The games he won against me. . . . Yet another glorious figure.
Plenty of others came by, less well-known perhaps , like Amand Gauthier, Rémy Ménard and [Emile-Louis]Mathon, who in his spare moments

sketched part of Michelangelo's *Last Judgment* in a small room at the bottom of the house — *en écorchés.*
(I was forgetting Claude Monet my pupil)
It was horrible! The Toutain boy, a colossus, died there in a fit of delirium tremens, thrown into a panic by these flayed fellows gasping for breath. Later on, Mère Toutain had those blood-coloured frescoes whitewashed over. I haven't even mentioned the last tenants like Gille [sic] and good old Cals, but all those memories have faded. Yet the joyful village fêtes I saw there some forty years ago, at a time when those sailor folk were still gay and people would dance after emptying a jar of beer. When it cost six sous a jar! I'm pleased to see people are busy bringing together a few memories of our old town of Honfleu [sic]. A small local Museum could be put together at once I think.
Above all, someone should search out a few paintings by Hamelin, whom you appear not to think very highly of, nor accord the rank he deserves. Yet he's the foremost of us all. He left some small marvels of painting, especially portraits. . . . I've preserved two of them that I've earmarked for the projected Museum, which will be its pearl.
It would be possible, moreover, for someone active and devoted to the *oeuvre* in question to find a number of portraits in Honfleur, for Hamelin did a lot of them — for free, what's more — and I really do feel that few people appreciate their merits.
He also made some wonderful drawings, comparable to those of his master, Ingres! And what a fine, honest man he was. What an artist!
You could do a lot, you who wield a suitably sharp pen, for our poor old town, which is rather too abandoned to its fate of a region *stuck in the mud* . . . and which, unlike its neighbour Trouville, doesn't see a river of gold running through its streets, but does have, to console itself, a full-bodied and very interesting historic past and can, moreover, be proud of a number of its children.

I'm hanging on to your journal, which conjures up memories of a hundred things already forgotten since those years when I lived in my 'bewitched' *pavillon* with its 36 steps — rue de l'Homme de Bois. . . .

(The bottom of the fifth page of Boudin's letter is missing; the tops of the words '. . . often the visit of. . .' can be made out on the next line.)

. . . he, too, came many times to get drunk on our good old Norman cider. Poor little house, I didn't have much money in the days I spent there either.

Finally, dear region, I have the small painting of the Washerwomen at your disposal, unfortunately I don't know how to get it to you, for I've only a few days left to stay in Deauville and don't know if I shall have the pleasure of seeing you
(The end of the page and letter are missing)

47 SERVANT OUTSIDE THE FERME
SAINT-SIMÉON, HONFLEUR, c. 1854–1857

Oil on board backed onto oak, 28.2 x 22.5 cm.
Unsigned, n.d., annotated top left *'La ferme
St-Siméon'*, monogram bottom right 'E. B.'
Eugène Boudin bequest, 1899 (Inv. 899-1-24)

Exhibition
1956 Galerie Katia Granoff, Paris, cat. n° 6

Bibliography
Catalogues of the Musée Eugène Boudin,
edition 1959 (n° 80)
R. Schmit, 1973, vol. I, n° 107

*Separated in 1954. This painting was found
on the back of* Tables at the Ferme Saint-
Siméon *(cat. 50).*

Servant outside the Ferme Saint-Siméon, Honfleur,
c. 1854–1857

CAT. 47

People Drinking at the Ferme Saint-Siméon, Honfleur
c. 1859

CAT. 48

48 PEOPLE DRINKING AT THE FERME SAINT-SIMÉON, HONFLEUR, c. 1859

Oil on board pasted onto poplar wood,
13 x 23.4 cm.
Signed bottom right 'E. Boudin', inscribed on
the back in ink 'Eugène Boudin'
Désiré Louveau bequest, 1937 (Inv. 937-1-3)

Exhibitions
1953 Mairie de Honfleur
1956 Galerie Katia Granoff, Paris, cat. n° 3
1976–1977 Smith College Museum of Art,
Northampton, and Clark Art Institute,
Williamstown (USA), cat. n° 38 (ill. p. 70)

Bibliography
Catalogue of the Musée Eugène Boudin,
edition 1959 (n° 81)
R. Schmit, 1973, vol. I, n° 150
Y. Le Pichon, *Les Peintres du Bonheur*, Paris, 1983,
p. 65

*'Half-way along is the Ferme Saint-Siméon.
A true farm, I can vouch for this, and in the most
ravishing spot in the world. A hedge as high as
a man shelters the surrounding area. One enters
a Norman courtyard, of the kind [Jules] Dupré,
Flers, Français, and a few other naturists
appreciated by the public know how to depict:
apple-trees here, hens there—with Manon,
a black she-ass, and a doe-eyed cow called
Toinette. A few tables, rooted to the spot,
are strewn with a profusion that becomes
parsimoniousness in the fine days of summer,
when jolly fishermen flock to empty sparkling
jugs of cider. . . .' (Alfred Delvau, Le Figaro,
8 January, 1865)*

110

Study of a Tree
c. 1853–1856

CAT. 49

Tables at the Ferme Saint-Siméon, Honfleur
c. 1859

49 STUDY OF A TREE, c. 1853–1856

Oil on board, 27.4 x 16 cm.
Unsigned
Inscribed on the back with a pen 'Eug.
Boudin—Louveau'
Désiré Louveau bequest, 1937 (Inv. 937-1-5)

Bibliography
Catalogues of the Musée Eugène Boudin,
1959 (n° 250)
R. Schmit, 1973, vol. I, n° 31

50 TABLES AT THE FERME SAINT-SIMÉON,
HONFLEUR, c. 1859

Oil on board backed onto oak, 22.5 x 28.4 cm.
Signed bottom left 'E. Boudin'
Eugène Boudin bequest, 1899 (Inv. 899-1-23)

Exhibition
1956 Galerie Katia Granoff, Paris, cat. n° 5

Bibliography
Catalogue of the Musée Eugène Boudin, 1959
(n° 71)
R. Schmit, 1973, vol. I, n° 30

*Separated in 1954. This painting was found
on the back of* Servant in front of the
Ferme Saint-Siméon *(cat. 47)*

51 PEOPLE RESTING BENEATH THE TREES, SAINT-
SIMÉON INN, HONFLEUR, c. 1854–1859

Pastel on blue paper, 14 x 21 cm.
Monogram bottom right 'E.B.'
Eugène Boudin bequest, 1899 (Inv. 899-1-45)

Exhibitions
1899 École Nationale des Beaux-Arts, Paris
1956 Galerie Katia Granoff, Paris, cat. n° 43.2
1992 Musée Eugène Boudin and Grenier à Sel,
Honfleur, cat. n° 247

Bibliography
Catalogues of the Musée Eugène Boudin,
1911 (n° 170), 1959 (n° 25)
Y. Le Pichon, *Les Peintres du Bonheur,* Paris,
1983, p. 67
J.-L. Ferrier, *L'Aventure de l'Art au XIXe Siècle,*
Paris, 1990, p. 503

52 PEOPLE DRINKING BENEATH THE TREES AT THE
FERME SAINT-SIMÉON, HONFLEUR, c. 1854–1859

Pastel on blue paper, 13.7 x 21.5 cm.
Monogram bottom right 'E.B.'
Eugène Boudin bequest, 1899 (Inv. 899-1-47)

Exhibitions
1899 École Nationale des Beaux-Arts, Paris
1956 Galerie Katia Granoff, Paris, cat. n° 43.4
1992 Musée Eugène Boudin and Grenier à Sel,
Honfleur, cat. n° 249

Bibliography
Catalogues of the Musée Eugène Boudin,
1911 (n° 170), 1959 (n° 25)

People Resting beneath the Trees, Saint-Siméon Inn Honfleur,
c. 1854–1859

53 TWO WOMEN AT TABLE AND FOWL AT THE
FERME SAINT-SIMÉON, HONFLEUR, c. 1854–1859

Pastel on blue paper, 13.7 x 21.2 cm.
Monogram bottom left 'E.B.'
Eugène Boudin bequest, 1899 (Inv. 899-1-48)

Exhibitions
1899 École Nationale des Beaux-Arts, Paris
1956 Galerie Katia Granoff, Paris, cat. n° 43.5
1992 Musée Eugène Boudin and Grenier à Sel,
Honfleur, cat. n° 250

Bibliography
Catalogues of the Musée Eugène Boudin,
1911 (n° 170), 1959 (n° 25)

54 PEOPLE DRINKING BENEATH THE TREES OUTSIDE
THE FERME SAINT -SIMÉON, HONFLEUR, c. 1854–1859

Pastel on blue paper, 15 x 21.2 cm.
Monogram bottom right 'E.B.'
Eugène Boudin bequest, 1899 (Inv. 899-1-46)

Exhibitions
1899 École Nationale des Beaux-Arts, Paris
1956 Galerie Katia Granoff, Paris, cat. n° 43.3
1992 Musée Eugène Boudin and Grenier à Sel,
Honfleur, cat. n° 248

Bibliography
Catalogues of the Musée Eugène Boudin, 1911
(n° 170), 1959 (n° 25), 1993 (p. 62)

People Drinking beneath the Trees at the Ferme Saint-Siméon, Honfleur
c. 1854–1859

CAT. 52

Two Women at Table and Fowl at the Ferme Saint-Siméon, Honfleur
c. 1854–1859

People Drinking beneath the Trees outside the Ferme Saint-Siméon, Honfleur
c. 1854–1859

55 Figures Sitting in Front of a Building
at the Ferme Saint-Siméon, Honfleur,
c. 1854–1859

Pastel on blue paper, 13.8 x 21.3 cm.
Monogram bottom left 'E.B.'
Eugène Boudin bequest, 1899 (Inv. 899-1-49)

Exhibitions
1899 École Nationale des Beaux-Arts, Paris
1956 Galerie Katia Granoff, Paris, cat. n° 43.6
1992 Musée Eugène Boudin and Grenier à Sel,
Honfleur, cat. n° 251

Bibliography
Catalogues of the Musée Eugène Boudin,
1911 (n° 170), 1959 (n° 25)

*Figures Sitting in front of a Building at the Ferme
Saint-Siméon, Honfleur, c. 1854–1859*

Cat. 55

56 Woman Breast-Feeding, Saint-Siméon Inn,
Honfleur, c. 1854–1859

Pastel on blue paper, 13.7 x 21.3 cm.
Monogram bottom right 'E.B.'
Eugène Boudin bequest, 1899 (Inv. 899-1-44)

Exhibitions
1899 École Nationale des Beaux-Arts, Paris
1956 Galerie Katia Granoff, Paris, cat. n° 43.1
1992 Musée Eugène Boudin and Grenier à Sel,
Honfleur, cat. n° 246

Bibliography
Catalogues of the Musée Eugène Boudin,
1911 (n° 170), 1959 (n° 25)

Woman Breast-Feeding, Saint-Siméon Inn, Honfleur
c. 1854–1859

Cat. 56

The Côte de Grâce – Figures in a Landscape

57 THE TROUVILLE ROAD (NEAR LE BUTIN), HONFLEUR, c. 1860–1863

Oil on canvas, 57 x 83 cm.
Signed bottom right 'E. Boudin'
Gift of Pablo Ispenian, 1959, in memory of
Jean Hallaure, born Le Havre 1886, died 1961
(Inv. 959-3-1)

Exhibitions
1978 Musée de l'Ancien Evêché, Évreux, cat.
ill. p. 36
1989 Musée de l'Evêché, Limoges, cat. n° 5
(ill. p. 30)
1992 Musée Eugène Boudin and Grenier à Sel,
Honfleur, cat. n° 20 (ill. p. 37)
1992–1993 Glasgow Museums, cat. n° 85 (ill.
p. 130)
1996–1997 (Japan) Bunkamura Museum of
Art, Tokyo,
Mie Prefectural Museum of Art, Tsu
Museum of Modern Art, Mito, Ibaraki

Bibliography
R. Schmit, 1973, vol. I, n° 5
L. Manœuvre, *Eugène Boudin et la Normandie*,
1991, p. 16
G. Papertian and B. Tréhet, *Normandie, Terre
des Arts*, Saussey, 1993, p. 32

*According to Laurent Manœuvre,
c. 1860–1863 is an improvement on the
previous dating (c. 1850–1855 or
1855–1858). The new dating is based on
studies of works from the same period and on
Boudin's treatment of the sky, which is
similar to that of the pastel studies seen by
Baudelaire in 1859 and now preserved at the
museum. The old Trouville road runs gently
down from the Saint-Siméon Inn towards the
shore. The road is today skirted by the
boulevard Charles V which runs along the
Seine on land won back from the river.*

58 BEECH GROVE AT THE CÔTE DE GRÂCE, HONFLEUR, c. 1860–1865

Oil on board, rounded corners, 26 x 40 cm.
Monogram bottom right 'E.B.' and illegible
date ['61' or '65']
Désiré Louveau bequest, 1937 (Inv. 937-1-7)

Exhibitions
1984–1985 (Japan) Sendai, Sapporo, Tokyo,
Nagoya, cat. n° 4
1992 Musée Eugène Boudin and Grenier à Sel,
Honfleur, cat. n° 6

Bibliography
Catalogues of the Musée Eugène Boudin,
1959 (n° 249)
R. Schmit, 1973, vol. I, n° 32

*These beech trees at the Côte de Grâce were
painted by a great many artists, among whom
Louis Français, who presented* Beech Trees at
the Côte de Grâce — Sunset *(Musée des
Beaux-Arts, Bordeaux) at the Salon of 1859.*

The Trouville Road (near Le Butin), Honfleur
c. 1860–1863

Beech Grove at the Côte de Grâce, Honfleur
c. 1860–1865

CAT. 58

The Beech Trees at the Côte de Grâce, Honfleur
c. 1853–1856

Cat. 59

59 THE BEECH TREES AT THE CÔTE DE GRÂCE, HONFLEUR, c. 1853–1856

Oil on poplar panel (in two parts),
30 x 30 cm.
Unsigned, inscribed on frame *'Offert par E. Boudin en 1896'*
Inscribed on the back in ink 'Eugène Boudin, les hêtres de la côte de Grâce' and stamped 'collection Louveau. Honfleur'
Désiré Louveau bequest, 1937 (Inv. 937-1-6)

Bibliography
Catalogues of the Musée Eugène Boudin, 1959 (n° 252)
R. Schmit, 1973, vol. I, n° 43

60 COWS AT THE CÔTE DE GRÂCE, HONFLEUR, 1856

Oil on board, 11.7 x 21.3 cm.
Signed and dated on the back 'E. Boudin 1886'
Inscribed on the back in pencil *'E.B. 1856, les arbres côte de Grâce'* and in ink 'Eugène Boudin 1856'
Désiré Louveau bequest, 1937 (Inv. 937-1-4)

Bibliography
Catalogues of the Musée Eugène Boudin, 1959 (n° 251)

61 PATH THROUGH THE WOODS, CÔTE DE GRÂCE, HONFLEUR, c. 1853–1856

Oil on board, 22.5 x 27 cm.
Inscribed on the back in ink *'Eugène Boudin, don de son frère Louis'*
Gift of Louis Boudin, 1899 (Inv. 899-2-1)

Bibliography
R. Schmit, 1973, vol. I, n° 3

*Cows at the Côte
de Grâce, Honfleur,
1856*

CAT. 60

*Path through
the Woods, Côte
de Grâce, Honfleur,
c. 1853–1856*

CAT. 61

62 NORMAN WOMAN SITTING IN THE GRASS,
c. 1857–1860

Oil on panel, 27 x 20.7 cm.
Unsigned, n.d.
Eugène Boudin bequest, 1899 (Inv. 899-1-2)

Exhibitions
1953 Mairie de Honfleur, cat. n° 28
1956 Galerie Katia Granoff, Paris, cat. n° 4
1992 Musée Eugène Boudin and Grenier à Sel,
Honfleur, cat. n° 13

Bibliography
Catalogues of the Musée Eugène Boudin,
1911 (n° 30), 1959 (n° 66), 1983 (p. 42)
R. Schmit, 1973, vol. I, n° 212
Y. Le Pichon, *Les Peintres du Bonheur*, Paris,
1983, p. 62

*This scene seems to be located on the Plateau
de Grâce de Honfleur, near the estuary and
the Ferme Saint-Siméon.*

63 FIGURES ON THE EDGE OF A WOOD, c. 1880

Oil on canvas, 36 x 58 cm.
Unsigned, n.d.
Eugène Boudin bequest, 1899 (Inv. 899-1-8)

Exhibitions
1953 Mairie de Honfleur, cat. n° 30
1956 Galerie Katia Granoff, Paris, cat. n° 24
1983 Fondation Prouvost, Marcq-en-Barœul,
cat. n° 73

1984-1985 (Japan) Sendai, Sapporo, Tokyo,
Nagoya, cat. n° 6

Bibliography
Catalogues of the Musée Eugène Boudin,
1911 (n° 27), 1959 (n° 65)
R. L. Benjamin, *Eugène Boudin*, Paris, 1937,
p. 181
R. Schmit, 1973, vol. I, n° 1203

64 LANDSCAPE WITH FIGURES, c. 1880

Oil on mahogany panel, 26.5 x 35.2 cm.
Unsigned, n.d.
Eugène Boudin bequest, 1899 (Inv. 899-1-7)

Exhibitions
1956 Galerie Katia Granoff, Paris, cat. n° 20
1970–1971 Leningrad, Moscow, Madrid

Bibliography
Catalogues of the Musée Eugène Boudin,
1911 (n° 24), 1959 (n° 82)
R. Schmit, 1973, vol. II, n° 1444
Videodisk, Musées de Basse-Normandie, 1994

*The figures in this painting have not been
identified. The woman on the left may be
Mme Boudin, and the work may be compared
to* Seated Woman in a Landscape, *dated
1880 (cat. 65). The other woman and two
children are certainly not Mme Monet, Jean
and Michel, as was long thought to be the
case.*

Norman Woman Sitting in the Grass
c. 1857–1860

Figures on the Edge of a Wood
c. 1880

Landscape with Figures
c. 1880

<small>CAT. 64</small>

65 SEATED WOMAN IN A LANDSCAPE, 1880

Oil on poplar-wood panel, 13.1 x 16.9 cm.
Monogram and date bottom right *'E.B. 1880 Juin'*
Eugène Boudin bequest, 1899 (Inv. 899-1-52)

Exhibitions
1956 Galerie Katia Granoff, Paris, cat. n° 21
1992 Musée Eugène Boudin and Grenier à Sel,
Honfleur, cat. n° 79

Bibliography
Catalogues of the Musée Eugène Boudin, 1911
(n° 32), 1959 (n° 74)
R. Schmit, 1973, vol. II, n° 1339

---

*The model's face is similar to that of Marie-Anne
Boudin, a portrait of whom is preserved in a private
collection (Schmit, 1451). The Boudin bequest in
Honfleur contains enough intimate works to justify
identifying the model as Marie-Anne. The woman
bears a strong resemblance to one of the two models
for* Landscape with Figures *(cat. 64). The
composition is very similar to that of a small panel
of 1878 representing another brown-haired woman,*
Madame Jacquette Sitting Reading at
Fervaques *(Schmidt, 3924).*

66 MADAME PÉCRUS IN HER GARDEN, c. 1878

Oil on mahogany panel, 23.5 x 13.7 cm.
Unsigned, n.d.
Eugène Boudin bequest, 1899 (Inv. 899-1-4)

Exhibitions
1956 Galerie Katia Granoff, Paris. Cat. n° 18
1976–1977 (USA) Smith College Museum of Art,
Northampton
Clark Art Institute, Williamstown, cat. n° 43. (ill.
p. 75)
1980 Musée de St-Maur des Fossés
1992 Musée Eugène Boudin and Grenier à Sel,
Honfleur, cat. n° 74

Bibliography
Catalogues du Musée Eugène Boudin, editions
1911 (n° 21), 1959 (n° 88).
L. Cario,1928, pl. 25
R. L. Benjamin, *Eugène Boudin*, 1937, p. 180
R. Schmit, 1973, vol. II, n° 1244

---

*In 1879, the painter Charles Pécrus (1826–1907)
made a portrait of Marie-Anne Boudin (cat. VIII),
while Boudin painted one of Mme Pécrus. These
two portraits imply a degree of intimacy between
the two men. There is also a version of Boudin's
portrait of Mme Pécrus that was made by Pécrus
himself and was almost certainly painted at the
same time (private collection). Boudin painted from
closer up and provides a more synthetic vision
which brings out the play of light on the materials.
In 1866, Pécrus moved into 42 rue Fontaine-Saint-
Georges (Boudin had been living at number 31
since 1864). The two painters may have met
around this time. In June 1883, Pécrus bought a*
Study of a Beach. *from Boudin. Pécrus was
originally given to more anecdotal subjects than
Boudin, but after the latter's death specialised in
themes dear to his friend:* Normandy Cows in
the Touques Valley *(Salon of 1900),* The Port at
Honfleur *(Salon of 1901),* The Commercial
Dock at Le Havre *(Salon of 1902) and* Berck-
Plage *(Salon of 1903).*

Seated Woman in a Landscape
1880

Cat. 65

Madame Pécrus in her Garden
c. 1878

CAT. 66

67 PORTRAIT OF A SMALL GIRL, c. 1880

Oil on mahogany panel, 29.3 x 21.7 cm.
Unsigned, n.d.
Eugène Boudin bequest, 1899 (Inv. 899-1-3)

Exhibitions
1956 Galerie Katia Granoff, Paris, cat. n° 23
1988, Musée des Beaux-Arts, Caen, cat. n° 25
(ill.p. 33)
1992 Musée Eugène Boudin and Grenier à Sel,
Honfleur, cat. n° 82 (ill. p. 186)
1993 Hôtel de Ville, Aulnay-sous-Bois,
cat. n° 38 (ill. p. 79)

Bibliography
Catalogues of the Musée Eugène Boudin,
1911 (n° 31), 1959 (n° 87), 1993 (p. 17)
L. Cario, 1928, pl. 24
R. L. Benjamin, *Eugène Boudin*, Paris, 1937,
p. 180
R. Schmit, 1973, vol. II, n° 1450

Portrait of a Small Girl
c. 1880

4 THE TOUQUES VALLEY

The river Touques has its source in the Orne, some nine kilometers from Gacé, from where it winds its way through the Calvados before flowing into the Channel between Trouville and Deauville.[1] Its right bank is dotted with houses that have sprung up along its 108-kilometer course. As a Gallic and Gallo-Roman waterway, the Touques possessed a number of ports, the most active of which, up until the 3rd century, was Lisieux, where a Gallic port was discovered during excavations of the cathedral square. In addition to Lisieux, the Touques flows through other old market-towns, such as Fervaques and Pont-l'Evêque, whose prosperity was reaffirmed in the 19th century thanks to their rich pasture-lands irrigated by the river.

It was in the valley and villages of the Touques that Boudin placed his easel, painting the same spots for forty years in his desire to try and render the instantaneous and atmospheric effects of sites he was knew well but would rediscover in a different light. The landscapes along the Touques were sufficiently varied to satisfy his wishes.

For the most part, the cattle grazing there are little more than components in a green landscape, pretexts for research into light and colour, like the strollers and fishermen in Boudin's beach scenes. Boudin had always shown an interest in these animals and, as a young painter, had admired the meadows painted by Potter, Dupré and Troyon. He was already depicting cattle along the estuary near Honfleur in the 1850s, but, between 1880 and 1896, would step up his studies of the Touques valley, above all seeking to render the effect of coloured volumes in light.

The Touques also afforded 'pure' landscapes, lush green banks bordering the river which sometimes broke its banks or formed marshland. Boudin made several paintings of the Deauville river, a branch of the Touques that was later severed and abandoned when the railway line was created. Boudin took advantage of the landscape to juxtapose sometimes crude greens and silvery greys under leaden, stormy skies, or skies washed clean by rain; a few small touches of colour indicate the presence of a fisherman, boat or person out strolling.

Of the villages through which the Touques flows, Boudin says very little. He disregarded Lisieux in his work, though he acknowledged the town's interest. Pont-l'Evêque and the steeple of the church of Saint-Michel occasionally turn up in

[1] 'En suivant la Touques', in *Athena sur la Touques*, n° 106–107, December 1990–March 1991.

drawings. On several occasions he worked in Touques itself. Most of his painting, however, was done at Fervaques, where he was detained by a friend, Dr. Jacquette; a few views exist of the village and the house where he stayed.[2] The Touques ends its life in Trouville. It was a subject Boudin never tired of and he devoted more than 200 paintings to the entrance to the jetties at high and low tide. Fishing boats and big sailing ships come and go in these seascapes, where the handling of water and sky gets the lion's share. It was likewise at the entrance to the jetties that, in 1894, Paul Helleu captured Boudin's silhouette in a number of dry-point engravings of the artist at work (cat. IV).

Another favourite subject of Boudin's was washerwomen, whom he painted many times as moving splashes of colour on the banks near the mouth of the river or the bridge over the Touques. The more than hundred paintings he made after 1866 make these a 'motif' on a par with the 'crinolines' in his beach scenes.

The constant presence of all these subjects in Boudin's work testifies both to the research he carried out and to changes in his style and perception. One notices, however, that it was only after 1878–1880 that Boudin began treating them more like 'series'; during a period, that is to say, when his financial worries were on the wane (thanks, among other things, to Durand-Ruel's help) and he had a house built in Deauville (1884). This confirms the appeal of his native region as a source of inspiration and a crucial element in his emotional stability.

The museum owns several works that are of significance for this chapter. The view of the main square in Fervaques (cat. 68) evokes the bustle of the large market-towns on the Touques. Works depicting herds in the valley (cat. 69 and 71) are a good example of the artist's varied graphic style. Boudin ran his practised eye over one animal after another, individualising each subject and treating it either in delicate detail or with quick splashes and brush-strokes. As for the painting of the entrance to the jetties at Trouville (cat. 72), the work, composed at low-tide, gives a good idea of the place, with its cloud-filled sky reflected in the water. The red and orange splashes of the fishing boats light up the tender, water-swept atmosphere of the port.

[2.] May 1869: first mention of Jacquette in the account books, with further mentions of Jacquette and her stays in Fervaques in summer 1874, October 1877, November 1879, November 1881 and July 1897.

68 FERVAQUES, 1882

Oil on mahogany panel, 23.2 x 24.5 cm.
Unsigned, date and location bottom right
'Fervaques 82'
Eugène Boudin bequest, 1899 (Inv. 899-1-9)

Exhibitions
1939 Rockefeller Center, New York
1952 Mairie de Honfleur
1956 Galerie Katia Granoff, Paris, cat. n° 27
1980 Fondation Prouvost, Marcq-en-Barœul,
cat. n° 27
1992 Musée Eugène Boudin and Grenier à Sel,
Honfleur, cat. n° 95

Bibliography
Catalogues of the Musée Eugène Boudin, 1911
(n° 22), 1959 (n° 85)
R. L. Benjamin, *Eugène Boudin,* Paris, 1937, p. 180
R. Schmit, 1973, vol. II, n° 1689

Between 1878 and 1882, Eugène Boudin painted four views of the village of Fervaques (entrance, street and square). The most interesting of these are the two views at the Musée Eugène Boudin and the Musée de Bayeux, showing the architecture and bustle of the market-town. Boudin also made paintings in Fervaques of Dr. Jacquette's house, Mme Jacquette, gardens and a farmyard.

Henri Michel-Lévy
*The Painter Boudin Painting Animals
in the Meadow at Deauville,* 1880

136

Fervaques
1882

CAT. 68

137

69 COWS IN THE TOUQUES VALLEY,
c. 1881–1887

Oil on canvas, 32.3 x 45.3 cm.
Unsigned
Gift of Mme Katia Granoff, 1959
(Inv. 959-5-1)

Exhibitions
1944 Galerie Charpentier, Paris
1992 Musée Eugène Boudin and Grenier à Sel,
Honfleur, cat. n° 89 (ill. p. 139)

Bibliography
R. Schmit, 1973, vol. II, n° 1483

*Boudin creates depth here by skilfully
dissolving the outlines, which become
increasingly less precise as the forms grow
distant from the observer. His technique also
underscores the sense of movement and light.
This work, then, is a résumé of pictorial
techniques, ranging from a light style of
drawing that respects the animal's anatomy
to a very modern 'tachism' used to suggest
volumes and their mobility in light.*

70 HORSE IN A STABLE, c. 1885–1890

Oil on mahogany panel, 32 x 41 cm.
Unsigned, n.d.
Eugène Boudin bequest, 1899 (Inv. 899-1-22)

Exhibitions
1956 Galerie Katia Granoff, Paris, cat. n° 16
1992 Musée Eugène Boudin and Grenier à Sel,
Honfleur, cat. n° 92

Bibliography
Catalogues of the Musée Eugène Boudin,
1911 (n° 15), 1959 (n° 86)
R. Schmit, 1973, vol. II, n° 1243

*Robert Schmit's catalogue raisonné lists
twenty-nine studies of horses over a twenty-
year period (c. 1875–1895). There is a
painting dated 1889 that is rather similar in
appearance to this one.*

Horse in a Stable, c. 1885–1890
CAT. 70

138

Cows in the Touques Valley,
c. 1881–1887

71 COWS IN A MEADOW, c. 1854–1862

Pastel on paper, 18 x 29.3 cm.
Stamped bottom right 'E.B.'
Hambourg-Rachet donation, 1988
(Inv. 988-1-3)

Exhibition
1992 Musée Eugène Boudin and Grenier à Sel,
Honfleur, cat. n° 255 (ill. p. 137)

Bibliography
*Donation Hambourg-Rachet au Musée Eugène
Boudin*, 1988, cat. n° 3, p. 34
L. Manœuvre, *Eugène Boudin, Drawings*, 1991,
p. 139

———————

This may be n° 279 of the studio sale, entitled
Animals at Pasture.

72 TROUVILLE, ENTRANCE TO THE JETTIES AT
LOW TIDE, c. 1888–1897

Oil on mahogany panel, 27 x 22.2 cm.
Signed bottom left 'E. Boudin'
Jacques Boussard bequest, 1990 (Inv. 990-2-1)

Exhibitions
1966 Galerie Max Kaganovitch, Paris
1992 Musée Eugène Boudin and Grenier à Sel,
Honfleur, cat. n° 123

Bibliography
Catalogue of the Musée Eugène Boudin, 1993
(p. 60)
R. Schmit, 1973, vol. II, n° 2352
Videodisk, Musées de Basse-Normandie, 1994

———————

*From 1881 till the end of his career, Boudin
regularly sold works similar in format and
subject to this one. It was in the early 1890s,
however, that his output for works of this kind
reached its height.*

Cows in a Meadow
c. 1854–1862

Cat. 71

Paul Helleu
*Eugène Boudin Painting on the Jetty
at Trouville,* 1894

Cat. IV

Anonymous
*Eugène Boudin Painting on the Jetty
at Trouville,* 1896

Cat. I

Trouville, Entrance to the Jetties at Low Tide
c. 1888–1897

<small>CAT. 72</small>

5 BRITTANY

by Laurent Manœuvre

Boudin enjoyed intermittent relations with Brittany. His feelings towards the region changed over the years, ranging back and forth from enthusiasm to disdain. At the beginning of his second voyage, he wrote: 'I'm in good health, rushing from one corner of Finistère to the next without being able to find one that suits me';[1] then: 'I've discovered the region too late, for it was the object of my dreams'.[2] Ten years later, he remarked: 'this region . . . has become a kind of home for us where everyone is a friend or acquaintance';[3] and finally: 'you've got to admit that anyone who longs only for the countryside, the little villages, the glad lands, can, in my view, stay put in our Normandy, which is every bit as fine as this side of Brittany'.[4] Boudin's first stays in Brittany (in 1855, but, above all, in 1857 and 1858) are known to us from his letters, paintings and a large number of drawings of undoubted ethnographic interest. Throughout this period, the young artist, shy and constantly dissatisfied, was still searching for an identity. Drawn to seascapes, he nevertheless conformed to the prevailing fashion for figure paintings and Breton exoticism. *The Pardon of Sainte-Anne-la-Palud* marks the high point of his attempt to fall in with the mood of the day.[5] Modelled on Rubens' *The Village Fête,*[6] the painting, exhibited at the Salon of 1859, is an example of anecdotal genre painting. The work was not up to the artist's ambitions, and Boudin took relevant stock of its failings: 'no centre, the interest is scattered . . . no breadth, no flexibility . . . a beginner's painting'.[7] Baudelaire, in his review of the Salon, dispenses with this 'very good and very sensible painting' in a few courteous words, using it as a pretext for a lengthy and subtle digression on Boudin's pastel studies of skies.[8] Despite appearences, *The Pardon of Sainte-Anne-la-Palud* was not a dead-end. In 1861, the poet Alphonse Darnault wrote to Boudin: 'I congratulate myself, then, on having summoned you to Finistère in the past; it was this trip that gave you a taste for figures'.[9] During the same period, this 'taste for figures' was perfectly fulfilled in Boudin's beach scenes, some of the earliest of which have a descriptive character similar to that of *The Pardon of Sainte-Anne-la-Palud.*
In 1863, Boudin married a Breton girl, Marie-Anne Guédès.[10] Four years later, he spent several weeks at his in-laws' home near Hôpital-Camfrout. Family matters aside, both this trip and that of the following year were made for a variety of reasons. The first of these was economic: 'our expenses are rather limited in this region where the food doesn't vary much'.[11] There were also health reasons, for the climate of Finistère seemed suited to the fragile constitution of Marie-Anne, who bathed, drank milk and ate pancakes 'to bursting'.[12] There were also painterly reasons, of course: 'it's a costly trip

1. Letter to his brother Louis, 12 July, 1857 (private collection).
2. Letter to his brother Louis, 14 July, 1857 (private collection).
3. Letter to Ferdinand Martin, 13 August, 1867 (Bibliothèque d'Art et d'Archéologie, Paris).
4. Letter to Ferdinand Martin, 7 July, 1868 (Bibliothèque d'Art et d'Archéologie, Paris).
5. Musée des Beaux-Arts André-Malraux, Le Havre.
6. Musée du Louvre, Paris.
7. Journal, January 1859 (Musée du Louvre, Paris).
8. Charles Baudelaire, *Curiosités Esthétiques,* Paris, 1931–1932.
9. Letter from Alphonse Darnault to Boudin, 15 December, 1861 (private collection).
10. Born 17 April, 1835, in Rusaden, near Hanvec. The marriage was held on 14 January, 1863, in Le Havre. The witnesses were Louis Boudin, the painter's brother, Ferdinand Martin and Louis-Alexandre Dubourg. According to the painter, the marriage took place in order to 'put things straight with society'. Boudin had been sharing his life with the woman he generally referred to as his 'companion' since 1859 (private journal, Musée du Louvre). The two young people may have met for the first time in 1856 ('visit from *la Bretonne*',

private journal, 12 October). Marie-Anne died in Paris on 24 March, 1889. She is buried near her husband in the Saint-Vincent cemetery in Montmartre.

11. Letter to Ferdinand Martin, 7 July, 1868 (Bibliothèque d'Art et d'Archéologie, Paris).

12. Letter to Ferdinand Martin, 13 August, 1867 (Bibliothèque d'Art et d'Archéologie, Paris).

13. Letter to Ferdinand Martin, 15 June, 1868 (Bibliothèque d'Art et d'Archéologie, Paris).

14. *Ibid.*

15. Letter to Ferdinand Martin, 21 July, 1867 (Bibliothèque d'Art et d'Archéologie, Paris).

16. Letter to Ferdinand Martin, 13 August, 1867 (Bibliothèque d'Art et d'Archéologie, Paris).

17. Letter to Ferdinand Martin, 21 July, 1867 (Bibliothèque d'Art et d'Archéologie, Paris).

18. Letter to Ferdinand Martin, 26 September, 1869 (Bibliothèque d'Art et d'Archéologie, Paris).

on our meagre resources but one must vary one's goods'.[13] Brittany was sufficiently exotic to provide a kind of 'last resort' for penniless artists: 'it's the other end of the world for us, yet it's less distant than Egypt or Persia, where at the moment Gérôme, Bonnat and so many other courageous explorers have gone'.[14]

During the 1860s, Boudin acquired great technical mastery: effects of light were faithfully observed, his touch became delicate and wiry, and his compositions were stripped of all superfluous matter. He also familiarised himself with watercolour, a light medium particularly suited to working from the motif. The artist applied the discoveries he had made on the coasts of the Channel to Brittany. Outlines are dissolved in light, forms reduced to mere splashes of colour. The rich colouring of the peasants' costumes is scarcely different from that of the clothes worn by people strolling at Trouville. As a lover of grey, Boudin used the granite of house fronts and church facades to bring out these vivid notes. Nevertheless, a number of works stand out and belong to Brittany alone: his interiors. The series dates from 1867 and came about for meteorological reasons: 'The weather, too, is very tiresome'.[15] Forced to work in 'cottages with deep shadows',[16] Boudin had to make do with the rare moments when the inhabitants were more or less still: 'it's also very difficult to get these little lads to pose, let alone the men, who only come home to eat'.[17] The few watercolours and Rembrandt-like paintings made at this time would not be followed up in his work. Just this once, Boudin, by nature more sensitive to subtle gradations than brutal oppositions, played on the violent contrasts between the shadowy light of the rooms and the whiteness of head-pieces and collars.

Once his brief infatuation with the rural world had passed, Boudin returned to his first loves: 'we remained by the sea out of preference, so as to continue in the maritime genre'.[18] The war of 1870 and the deaths of Marie-Anne's nearest and dearest, were to aggravate the rupture. Boudin took refuge first in Brussels, then in Antwerp. The interest the artist showed in these northern regions, and the demands of art-lovers, worked against Brittany. In 1872, Boudin settled in Camaret again, painting the bustle of the port and the sardine boats. The following year, he abandoned Finistère for the Côtes-d'Armor; in Portrieux, he took an interest in the Newfoundland fishermen. Brittany later underwent a long eclipse. In 1897, the artist undertook a last tour, from Le Croisic to the Pointe du Raz. The paintings he made at this time, marked by great freedom and a clear, powerful use of colour, along with some rather allusive drawings flooded with light, bring to a happy close a life dedicated to painting.

73 BRETON WOMAN KNITTING, c. 1865

Oil on board, 23.4 x 17.2 cm.
Unsigned, n.d.
Eugène Boudin bequest, 1899 (Inv. 899-1-6)

Exhibitions
1956 Galerie Katia Granoff, Paris, cat. n° 10
1964 Musée des Beaux-Arts, Rennes, cat. n°
35 (ill. p. 46)
1992 Musée Eugène Boudin and Grenier à Sel,
Honfleur, cat. n° 33

Bibliography
Catalogues of the Musée Eugène Boudin,
1911 (n° 28), 1959 (n° 64)
R. Schmit, 1973, vol. I, n° 365
D. Delouche, *Eugène Boudin et la Bretagne,*
Rennes, 1987, p. 47

*This has been painted over a partly visible
study of a landscape. The same model was used
for a painting dated 1865 (*Recollection of Le
Faou, *Schmit, 335). If we assume that the
portraits Boudin bequeathed to his native town
were those of his nearest and dearest and
friends, the model could be the sister of Marie-
Anne Guédès, who lived in Le Faou. Another
painting similar to this one represents a Breton
woman sewing in an interior and is dedicated
to Mme Ferdinand Martin (private collection,
Schmit, 368). Eight drawings from the same
period depicting Breton women sewing or
knitting are preserved at the Louvre (RF 17829,
17834, 17947, 17955, 17956, 18704, 18760,
18789).*

74 BRETON INTERIOR, c. 1867

Watercolour over graphite pencil sketch on
paper, highlights of white gouache, partly
oxidized, 22.5 x 30.5 cm.
Stamped bottom left, centre and right 'E.B.',
illegible annotation near lower edge
Hambourg-Rachet donation, 1988
(Inv. 988-1-6)

Exhibition
1992 Musée Eugène Boudin and Grenier à Sel,
Honfleur, cat. n° 298

Bibliography
*Donation Hambourg-Rachet au Musée Eugène
Boudin,* 1988, cat. n° 6 (ill. p. 29)
L. Manœuvre, *Eugène Boudin, Dessins,*
1991, p. 153

Breton Woman Knitting
c. 1865

75 BRETON WOMAN AND TWO CHILDREN, c. 1867

Watercolour with highlights of white and
black gouache over pencil sketch on brown
paper pasted onto board, 10.8 x 13.1 cm.
Piece missing at lower left corner and
some tears
Hambourg-Rachet donation, 1988
(Inv. 988-1-18)

Exhibition
1992 Musée Eugène Boudin and Grenier à Sel,
Honfleur, cat. n° 299

Bibliography
*Donation Hambourg-Rachet au Musée Eugène
Boudin*, 1988, cat. n° 18, p. 28

76 BRETON WOMAN IN AN INTERIOR, c. 1867

Watercolour with highlights of white
and black gouache over graphite pencil
and charcoal sketch on brown paper,
13.2 x 15.5 cm.
Hambourg-Rachet donation, 1988
(Inv. 988-1-17)

Exhibition
1992 Musée Eugène Boudin and Grenier à Sel,
Honfleur, cat. n° 300

Bibliography
*Donation Hambourg-Rachet au Musée Eugène
Boudin*, 1988, cat. n° 17, p. 28

Breton Interior
c. 1867

CAT. 74

Breton Woman and Two Children
c. 1867

Breton Woman in an Interior
c. 1867

6 THE BEACHES OF THE BAIE

DE SEINE and the shores of the North

'Monsieur Boudin . . . has even invented a genre of seascapes which is all his own, and which consists in painting along with the beach an exotic crowd of high society come together for the high life in summer in our spa-towns'.[1]

Some time around 1860, on the advice of Isabey or Martin,[2] Boudin embarked on a 'portrayal of manners' in which he depicted the crowd of city-dwellers on the beaches at Trouville and Deauville. These bathing resorts were new creations. Trouville, originally a fishermen's village, had been transformed around 1848, while Deauville had been created around 1861 by the duc de Morny. Accessible by rail after 1860, these towns accommodated the bourgeoisie of the Second Empire, and buildings sprung up everywhere: casinos, race courses, sumptuous villas and luxury hotels. The *catalogue raisonné* of Boudin's paintings[3] numbers nearly three hundred items on the theme of 'crinoline' beaches, out of a total of 4,050 paintings. Boudin treated the subject from 1860 to 1896, though his output fell off after 1880. After 1890, Boudin transformed the subject, turning his 'crinoline' beaches into vast seascapes with tiny silhouettes moving about in the distance. The theme seems to have brought him some measure of success, as Boudin confessed to Ferdinand Martin in 1863: 'people are very fond of my little ladies on the beach, some of them maintain they're a gold-mine that ought to be exploited'.[4] Martin, who acted as something of a go-between in Le Havre between the painter and his clients, immediately advised him: 'I think that if you take a little more care over the details of the toilet of your *élégantes* at Trouville, you might have some success, but don't muddle everything up; you know that women are meticulous about their toilet, and if you dress your bathers up all wrong, they won't turn their gaze to your skies, nor to your hazy distances, to excuse the carelessness of your brushwork when it comes to their parasols or head-gear.[5] In 1864, Alfred Cadart and Jules Luquet commissioned beach-scenes, and Boudin noted in his account books: 'beach-scenes with small numbers of carefully painted figures', in response to the wishes of his dealers. At the time (roughly between 1863 and 1865), Boudin was selling his small beach-scenes for between 100 and 150 francs apiece,[6] depending on format and type, for he distinguished between paintings and 'sketches' or 'studies' when identifying works he had sold. The individual sale price was sometimes lower when he delivered several paintings at once. In May 1864, for example, he sold five beach-scenes with figures and a jetty for 400 francs the lot.

In 1868, Boudin's friends echoed hostile criticism, accusing him of turning out these

1. Jules-Antoine Castagnary, *Salon de 1869.*

2. In a letter of 9 September, 1868, Martin claimed to be the father of beach painting: 'It was I who first urged you to do beach scenes. . . . But I gave you this advice six or eight years ago' (Gérard Jean-Aubry, manuscript notes, private collection).

3. .Robert and Manuel Schmit, 1993.

4. Gérard Jean-Aubry, 1968, p. 50.

5. Letter of 13 February, 1863 (Gérard Jean-Aubry, manuscript notes, private collection).

6. 100 francs was equivalent to roughly 1,850 francs in today's money.

fashionable subjects much too easily. Martin urged him 'very seriously to put aside for a moment your beaches at Trouville and return to your seascapes'[7] in which 'you're capable of giving a true impression of nature, and where you're free to introduce the human element'.[8] Boudin felt a need to justify himself. He replied to Martin: 'Your letter reached me just as I was showing Ribot, Bureau and another person my small studies of fashionable beaches. These gentlemen were congratulating me precisely for daring to include the objects and people of our day in my pictures, for finding a way of making gentlemen in overcoats and ladies in waterproofs acceptable, thanks to the dressing and presentation. Yet there's nothing new about this attempt, since all the Italians and Flemish did was paint the people of their times, either in interiors or in their vast structures; it's gaining ground, and many young people, foremost among whom I place Monet, think it an element that's been too looked-down-upon until now. The peasants have their favourite painters: Millet, Jacque, Breton, and that's fine; these people do serious work, they labour, they're bound up in the Creator's work, which they carry on by helping him manifest himself in a way that's fruitful for man. That's fine, but, between ourselves, don't these bourgeois strolling on the jetty near sunset have the right to be fixed on canvas, to be brought into the light? Between ourselves, they're often resting after toiling hard, these men who've just come from their offices and chambers. If there are some parasites among them, there are also men who've fulfilled their task, are there not? That is a serious and irrefutable argument'.[9] Nevertheless, over the years Boudin sometimes felt bored producing the beach scenes that art-lovers called for. He was to abandon these genre paintings on several occasions, but would confess with gratitude and honesty that, after so many years of uncertainty, he was grateful for the success enjoyed by his *'petites poupées'*.

The great majority of the three hundred beach-scenes Boudin made of the Baie de Seine were painted on wood, using small formats that he could easily use outdoors and then put away in a box fitted out for that purpose. Boudin worked from these small panels when executing big studio paintings, as well as from a large number of drawings, studies highlighted with watercolour and written annotations that served as *aide-mémoires*. Boudin presented beach-scenes with figures at the Paris Salon between 1864 and 1870, and at various exhibitions in the provinces between 1867 and 1870.[10] This is confirmation indeed of widespread public infatuation with the subject, and of the interest Boudin himself showed in it. It was his most prolific period.

7. Letter of 1 September, 1868 (Gérard Jean-Aubry, manuscript notes, private collection).

8. Letter of 9 September, 1868 (Gérard Jean-Aubry, manuscript notes, private collection).

9. Gérard Jean-Aubry, 1968, p. 72. A year later, on his return from Finistère on 28 August, 1867, Boudin sang the praises of 'these races devoted to the harsh labour of the fields, to black bread and water' and criticised 'this band of gilded parasites'.

10. Exhibitions in Versailles, Lyon, Pau, Le Havre, Strasbourg, Bordeaux, Brussels.

Boudin's paintings of beach scenes with city-dwellers are often composed in the same manner: a large upper register is reserved for the sky, while the lower third of the beach is filled with figures, seated or standing, in distinct groups or a continuous strip, seen either from behind or in profile. Beach and sea have only secondary importance compared to this foreground. As the series progresses, Boudin's vision and pictorial technique evolves. Initially concerned with analysing detail, he moves on to a more synthetic vision. The figures on the beach become receptive to the surrounding atmosphere that gives them their vitality. Forms and outlines vibrate with air and light. Scattered about the canvas are pure colours, such as blue, yellow and vermilion, skilfully arranged so as to enhance the beiges, greys and blacks. In 1883, Gustave Geffroy defined with great subtlety Boudin's technical and sensory innovations: 'He teaches us that there is no such thing as an opaque black, that air is transparent. He observes the values objects take on in light, and the manner in which planes are established as far as the horizon. He renders minute differences in the infinite and ravishing tonal range of greys. He captures the movements of things at the same time as their forms and colours'.[11] Around 1890, Boudin changed the style of his beach-scenes, no longer representing figures in close-up. He enlarged his field of vision, treating the beaches at Honfleur, Trouville and Deauville, Bénerville, Tourgéville and Villers like landscapes. In the natural environment formed by sea, sky and sand, the strolling figures, fishermen or horse-drawn carriages are small dark signs on a clear background.

The beaches of the Baie de Seine were among Boudin's favourite subjects, but he didn't limit himself to the region. He painted the beach at Sainte-Adresse, as well as that at Etretat which, being close to the cliffs, provided a safe haven for the fishing boats. After those of Normandy, Boudin's second love was the beaches of the North and Picardy. He rarely depicted the beaches at Cayeux or Saint-Valéry, preferring those at Etaples or Berck, where he made nearly a hundred paintings. Once again, the themes that preoccupied him were those of the fishermen, the fishermen's wives and the return of the fishing boats. Very few, only two or three perhaps, of the beach-scenes he painted at Berck had city-dwellers in them like those at Trouville. Boudin also discovered beach-scenes at Kerhor and Portrieux in Brittany, and at Scheveningen in Holland; and, once again, it was the fishermen who caught his attention. Boudin genuinely created a commonplace. He was one of the few to exploit the theme over such a long period (thirty-six years) and to devote so many works to it. Isabey, Dubourg, Pécrus, Lapostolet, Jongkind, Monet and Manet had all drawn on beaches for inspiration, of course, but only Boudin created a genre, a

11. *La Justice,* 15 February, 1883.

series even, in the manner of Monet. Boudin's beach-scenes are not a pretext for sociological study, they are a way of hunting out light, transparency and the expression of movement. 'Observe carefully and extract from nature everything that can be extracted. Above all, light! Seek its radiance, its flash, render it down, hunt out its warmth.'[12]

His paintings of people whiling away their time at the water's edge didn't make Boudin forget the coastal landscapes he had known since his youth in Honfleur and Le Havre. He paid homage to the work of the fishermen and the patience of the women who waited on the shore for the moment to unload the fish. Boudin had also been observing since childhood the large sailing ships and fishing boats that hugged the coasts before putting in at the docks of Honfleur and Le Havre, then later at Deauville. It was only natural that he should specialise in seascape painting, urged on by friends such as Monet, who in 1859 recommended: 'all in all, there's a total lack of seascape painters, and it's a path that would take you far'.[13] All through his life, Boudin composed seascapes or views of coastal areas and ports. Bordeaux, Portrieux, Le Havre, Honfleur, Fécamp, Dieppe, Antwerp, Brussels and the ports of the Midi were pretexts for representing great sailing ships — under threat from steam — small rowing boats and the bustle of the quays. The human presence is always there, reassuring and industrious.

The Musée Eugène Boudin, though it possesses a fine series of beach scenes painted between 1865 and 1884, has few seascapes. The two views of the ports at Antwerp (1871) and Dieppe (c. 1897) are nevertheless interesting. The view of the port at Antwerp is a 'history' painting, for it relates, unusually for Boudin, an event that occurred during his exile in Belgium. The historical pretext is not immediately apparent, however, for the colours and rendering of movement in the painting — which for a long time was known as *The Regattas at Antwerp* — give no inkling of the painful official repatriation of the remains of Dutch soldiers fallen at the siege of the citadel in 1832. As for the large seascape offered to the museum by Adrien Voisard-Margerie under the title *Port of Deauville* and now known as *Port of Dieppe,* it is one of the great works Boudin made during his last two years as a painter. During his trips to the Brittany and Normandy coasts in the summer of 1896 and 1897, Boudin produced clear paintings whose powerful sense of line reveal his modernity and great technical facility. The painting was originally 'given to a friend from Honfleur' (Désiré Louveau), then later offered by Madame Louveau to Adrien Voisard-Margerie, who was curator at the time and in turn bequeathed it to the museum at his death.

12. Gustave Cahen, 1900, p. 196.
13. Letter from Claude Monet to Eugène Boudin, 3 June, 1859, in Gérard Jean-Aubry, 1968, p. 35.

77 BEACH SCENE AT TROUVILLE, c. 1865–1867

Oil on board backed onto oak, 22.5 x 29.1 cm.
Unsigned, n.d.
Eugène Boudin bequest, 1899 (Inv. 899-1-11)

Exhibitions
1956 Galerie Katia Granoff, Paris, cat. n° 8
1992 Musée Eugène Boudin and Grenier à Sel,
Honfleur, cat. n° 35

Bibliography
Catalogues of the Musée Eugène Boudin,
1959 (n° 75), 1983 (p. 39), 1993 (p. 59)
R. Schmit, 1973, vol. I, n° 355
M. Howard, *Monet*, 1989, p. 6
La Basse-Normandie, Conseil Général de Basse-
Normandie, 1991, p. 51
Claude Monet, Tokyo, 1994
Videodisk, Musées de Basse-Normandie, 1994
Boudin at Trouville, Art Gallery and Museum,
Glasgow, 1993, n° 38
(ill. p. 77)
Peintres en Normandie, Saint-Lô, 1995, p. 51

*This beach scene was found on the back
of the portrait of Léonard-Sébastien Boudin
(cat. 14). It was separated and backed onto
oak in 1954. It is not sure that it was
painted at Trouville, but seems likely when
one considers the numerous beach scenes
Boudin painted at Trouville-Deauville
between 1863 and 1865. On 13 February,
1863, Ferdinand Martin wrote to Boudin: 'I
think that if you take a little more care over
the details of the toilet of your élégantes at
Trouville, you might have
some success'.*

78 BEACH SCENE AT TROUVILLE, 1878

Oil on mahogany panel, 14 x 26.2 cm.
Monogram, location and date bottom right
'3 7bre 78' [or 'B. Tlle 78']. The former
hypothesis is more plausible, however, as
Boudin never used the monogram 'B.', only
'E.B.']
Eugène Boudin bequest, 1899 (Inv. 899-1-14)

Exhibitions
1953 Mairie de Honfleur, cat. n° 24
1956 Galerie Katia Granoff, Paris, cat n° 9
1992 Musée Eugène Boudin and Grenier à Sel,
Honfleur, cat. n° 73

Bibliography
Catalogues of the Musée Eugène Boudin,
1911 (n° 17), 1959 (n° 77)
R. Schmit, 1973, vol. II, n° 1231

*Divided into horizontal bands, this painting
shows us women reading, conversing or
working on the beach, though none of them
shows any interest either in the painter who is
depicting them, nor in ourselves, the spectators.
As is often the case in Boudin's works, the
figures have their backs turned to us.*

Beach Scene at Trouville
c. 1865–1867

CAT. 77

161

Beach Scene at Trouville
c. 1865–1867

The Conversation on the Beach at Trouville
1876

<small>CAT. 79</small>

79 THE CONVERSATION ON THE BEACH
AT TROUVILLE, 1876

Oil on mahogany panel, 12.5 x 24.7 cm.
Signed bottom left 'E. Boudin', date and
location bottom right 'Trouville 76'
Eugène Boudin bequest, 1899 (Inv. 899-1-12)

Exhibitions
1939 Rockefeller Center, New York
1953 Mairie de Honfleur, cat. n° 26
1956 Galerie Katia Granoff, Paris, cat. n° 15
1992 Musée Eugène Boudin and Grenier à Sel,
Honfleur, cat. n° 71

Bibliography
Catalogues of the Musée Eugène Boudin, 1911
(n° 19), 1959 (n° 73), 1983 (p. 41), 1993 (p. 61)
R. L. Benjamin, *Eugène Boudin,* Paris, 1937,
p. 180
S. Fourny-Dargère, *Monet,* Paris, 1992, fig. 2,
p. 32
Mille Peintures des Musées de France, Paris, 1993,
p. 408
Y. Le Pichon, *Les Peintres du Bonheur,* Paris, 1993,
p. 78
R. Schmit, 1973, vol. I, n° 1141
Videodisk, Musées de Basse-Normandie, 1994
Peintres en Normandie, Saint-Lô, 1995, p. 22

---

*This is the only beach scene at Trouville dated
1876 that is currently known. In many of his
compositions, Boudin organised his figures in
groups. Here he uses a circle. To disrupt the
circular effect, however, he places a chair
outside the group, or sketches in one or
several more distant figures (cat. 80).
A splash of vermilion lights up the entire
painting. 'Try to make the relief flat but the
tone lively. Exaggerate very slightly to bring
out the whole. . . .' (Eugène Boudin, 1865, in
G. Cahen, 1900, p. 191). The splash of
vermilion is echoed by the small red ribbons
in the figures' hair and hats. The list of
paintings that Boudin bequeathed to his
native town includes a beach scene described
as measuring 11 x 24 cm. and entitled* A
Light Meal on the Beach with the Family
of the Painter Mettling. *The dimensions
of* The Conversation *(12.3 x 24.7 cm.)
suggest that it might be the 'light meal'
in question.*

80 BEACH SCENE AT TROUVILLE, 1880

Oil on mahogany panel, 21.5 x 35.5 cm.
Monogram, location and date bottom right
'E.B. Tlle [Trouville]. Octobre 1880'
Eugène Boudin bequest, 1899 (Inv. 899-1-13)

Exhibitions
1952 Mairie de Honfleur
1953 Mairie de Honfleur, cat. n° 23
1956 Galerie Katia Granoff, Paris, cat. n° 19
1992 Musée Eugène Boudin and Grenier à Sel,
Honfleur, cat. n° 78

Bibliography
Catalogues of the Musée Eugène Boudin, 1911
(n° 16), 1959 (n° 67)
R. L. Benjamin, *Eugène Boudin,* Paris, 1937,
p. 180
R. Schmit, 1973, vol. II, n° 1308

*The organisation of these beach scenes is often
identical: two approximately equal bands
representing sand and sky, and a middle zone
where the figures are placed facing the sea
(with or without boats). Here, the centre of the
composition is occupied by an empty chair on
which a yellow object (a bag) is placed. This
centre is further underscored by the yacht on
the sea. To either side are two women facing
one another, then figures spaced out along a
horizontal band closed off at either end by two
small boys who are turned towards us. The
composition is lit up by a skilful distribution
of vivid colours: vermilion, red and blue.*

81 WOMAN WITH PARASOL ON THE BEACH AT
BERCK, c. 1873–1880

Oil on poplar panel, 12.5 x 17.5 cm.
Eugène Boudin bequest, 1899 (Inv. 899-1-53)

Exhibitions
1956 Galerie Katia Granoff, Paris. Cat. n° 22
1992 Musée Eugène Boudin and Grenier à Sel,
Honfleur. Cat. n° 67 (ill. p. 170)

Bibliography
Catalogues of the Musée Eugène Boudin,
1911 (n° 18), 1959 (n° 76), 1983 (p. 37), 1993
(p. 58)
R. Schmit, 1973, vol. II, n° 1371
J. Selz, 1982, p. 76
Y. Le Pichon, *Les Peintres du Bonheur*, Paris,
1983, p. 82
P. Lurie, *Guide to the Impressionist Landscape*,
1990
L. Manœuvre, 1994 (back jacket)
Videodisk, Musées de Basse-Normandie, 1994
Postage stamp representing *Woman with a
Parasol*, date of issue, 23 May, 1987

*In the left-hand area, one can make out a
small boat of a kind that is typical of Berck
but more clearly legible on an almost identical
work (private collection, Schmit, 1372).
Boudin discovered Berck in 1873. If the
woman he has represented is Marie-Anne (as
the bequest of the work to the town of
Honfleur would suggest), she is either in
mourning for her mother (who died in 1871)
or her sister (who died in 1873). This would
mean the picture could be dated around the
time of Boudin's first stays at Berck. This
painting was formerly situated 'in Trouville'.*

Beach Scene at Trouville
1880

<small>Cat. 80</small>

Woman with Parasol on the Beach at Berck
c. 1873–1880

82 BEACH SCENE WITH SEATED MAN, c. 1865–1870

Watercolour over graphite pencil sketch on white paper pasted onto paper and board, 12.7 x 24.3 cm.
Stamped bottom right 'E.B.', illegible annotations on the drawing
Hambourg-Rachet donation, 1988
(Inv. 988-1-8)

Exhibitions
1965 Mairie de Trouville-sur-Mer
1992 Musée Eugène Boudin and Grenier à Sel, Honfleur, cat. n° 291

Bibliography
Donation Hambourg-Rachet au Musée Eugène Boudin, 1988, cat. n° 8 (ill. p. 31)
Catalogue of the Musée Eugène Boudin, 1993 (p. 103)
Videodisk, Musées de Basse-Normandie, 1994

'Watercolour isn't very difficult; it's a question of proceeding in an orderly fashion. You trace onto your paper, which comes in a block glued on three sides, a drawing with very clear lines, either in black pencil or graphite, and you fill in with colour, taking care to reserve the lights. One mustn't be afraid to work with vigour' (Letter from Boudin to Ferdinand Martin, 25 April, 1869). *'One mustn't be shy with colours; it's vitally important, in fact, that one exaggerate their brilliance'* (Letter to Martin, 14 June, 1869)

83 TROUVILLE, WOMEN AND CHILDREN OUTSIDE THE CASINO, c. 1884

Oil on beech panel, 22.2 x 42.2 cm.
Unsigned, n.d.
Eugène Boudin bequest, 1899 (Inv. 899-1-15)

Exhibitions
1953 Mairie de Honfleur, cat. n° 22
1956 Galerie Katia Granoff, Paris, cat. n° 13
1980 Fondation Prouvost, Marcq-en-Barœul, cat. n° 16
1988 Musée des Beaux-Arts, Caen, cat. n° 47 (ill. p. 47)
1992 Musée Eugène Boudin and Grenier à Sel, Honfleur, cat. n° 154
1992–1993 Glasgow Art Gallery and Museum

Bibliography
Catalogues of the Musée Eugène Boudin, 1911 (n° 25), 1959 (n° 79)
R. Schmit, 1973, vol. II, n° 1864
Y. Le Pichon, *Les Peintres du Bonheur,* Paris, 1983, p. 78
L. Manœuvre, 1994, pl. 36

This work is similar in style and format to cat. 84, likewise dated 1884. Both paintings illustrate themes dear to Boudin: a seated man reading a newspaper, seated women talking, groups of children forming light splashes on the sand, and nurses, young or old, wearing large aprons and bonnets. The bustle is marked by skilfully grouped brush-strokes and splashes, which create an illusion of mass and a sense of movement. These beach scenes, so spontaneous in appearance, are organised in successive planes that hollow out a sense of depth.

Beach Scene with Seated Man
c. 1865–1870

CAT. 82

Trouville, Women and Children outside the Casino
c. 1884

Figures outside the Tent of the Casino at Trouville
c.1884

84 FIGURES OUTSIDE THE TENT OF THE CASINO AT TROUVILLE, c. 1884

Oil on mahogany panel, 22.4 x 42.3 cm.
Signed and dated bottom right 'E. Boudin
26 Sept. 84'
Eugène Boudin bequest, 1899 (Inv. 899-1-16)

Exhibitions
1953 Mairie de Honfleur
1956 Galerie Katia Granoff, Paris, cat. n° 14
1958 Marlborough Fine Art, London
1965 Mairie de Trouville, cat. n° 10
1982 *Salon de la Société des Artistes Français,*
Grand Palais, Paris, cat. n° 35
1992 Musée Eugène Boudin and Grenier à Sel,
Honfleur, cat. n° 106 (ill. p. 93)
1993 Hôtel de Ville, Aulnay-sous-Bois,
cat. n° 18 (ill. p. 51)

Bibliography
Catalogues of the Musée Eugène Boudin, 1911
(n° 26), 1959 (n° 72)
R. L. Benjamin, *Eugène Boudin*, Paris, 1937, p. 181
R. Schmit, 1973, vol. II, n° 1897

Boudin often painted on panels of wood (made of oak or mahogany) for small and medium-sized formats. He explained his reasons for this choice of backing to his friend, the painter Braquaval, on 15 October, 1894: 'I think I'll go back to mahogany,
the only wood that's gentle, along with old oak. But mahogany is so heavy. And then
there's another drawback, it blackens even through primer when it isn't thick and several layers deep.'

85 THE ENGLISH FLEET COMES TO FETCH THE REMAINS OF SOLDIERS BURIED IN THE CITADEL OF ANTWERP, called THE REGATTAS OF ANTWERP, c. 1871

Oil on mahogany panel, 21 x 37.3 cm.
Unsigned, n.d.
Eugène Boudin bequest, 1899 (Inv. 899-1-10)

Exhibitions
1956 Galerie Katia Granoff, Paris, cat. n° 26
1992 Musée Eugène Boudin and Grenier à Sel,
Honfleur, cat. n° 50 (ill. p. 180)

Bibliography
Catalogues of the Musée Eugène Boudin,
1911 (n° 23, ill. p. 4 bis), 1959 (n° 69), 1983 (p. 38)
R. Schmit, 1973, vol. I, n° 755
J. Selz, 1982, p. 68 and back jacket
L. Manœuvre, *Boudin, le Ciel et la Mer*, 1994,
pl. 22
Videodisk, Musées de Basse-Normandie, 1994

This seems to be a sketch for a painting dated August 1871 and sold in an auction on 23 January, 1878, entitled The English Fleet Comes to Fetch the Remains of Soldiers Buried in the Citadel of Antwerp

(Schmit, 675). The composition at least is identical. The painting depicts the repatriation of the remains of Dutch soldiers fallen at Antwerp during the siege of the citadel in 1832. On 5 May, 1871, a royal decree authorised the Spanish citadel to be demolished to enlarge the port. The soldiers' remains were dug up and the Dutch steamship 'Valk' charged with transporting them, as was done on 21 August, 1871. Dutch and Belgian flags are fluttering on the quays and pier. (Information given in March 1976 by M. J. Van Elewyck, deputy burgomaster of the city of Antwerp and member of the Belgian parliament).

86	Pᴏʀᴛ ᴏꜰ ᴅɪᴇᴘᴘᴇ, 1896

Oil on canvas, 65 x 92 cm.
Unsigned
Adrien Voisard-Margerie bequest, 1954
(Inv. 954-1-2)

Exhibitions
1956 Galerie Katia Granoff, Paris, cat. n° 29
1992 Musée Eugène Boudin and Grenier à Sel, Honfleur, cat. n° 166 (ill. p. 130)

Bibliography
Catalogue of the Musée Eugène Boudin, 1959 (n° 89)
R. Schmit, 1973, vol. III, n° 3052
J. Selz, 1982, p. 90

S. Malcolm, *100 of the World's Most Beautiful Paintings*, New York, 1991, p. 54

This work was probably painted in late August-early September 1896, like the rest of the series dated by Robert Schmit to 1892–1896 (Schmit, 3051–3056). The more highly developed works in this series were likewise sold before the artist's death. The remainder were either given by Boudin to friends or sold in 1899. This painting was originally given to a friend from Honfleur, Louveau, in 1896 (account book, archives), then given by Mme Désiré Louveau to Adrien Voisard-Margerie, who bequeathed it to the museum in 1954. Voisard-Margerie was curator of the Musée Eugène Boudin from 1930 to 1953.

The English Fleet Comes to Fetch the Remains of Soldiers Buried in the Citadel of Antwerp,
called *Regattas at Antwerp,* c. 1871

CAT. 85

Port of Dieppe
1896

CAT. 86

87 FISHERWOMAN AT BERCK, 1886

Oil on poplar panel, 24.1 x 18.8 cm.
Monogram, location and date bottom middle
'E.B. Berck 86'
The back has been used as a palette
Eugène Boudin bequest, 1899 (Inv. 899-1-5)

Exhibitions
1956 Galerie Katia Granoff, Paris, cat. n° 28
1980 Fondation Prouvost, Marcq-en-Barœul,
cat. n° 31
1992 Musée Eugène Boudin and Grenier à Sel,
Honfleur, cat. n° 116

Bibliography
Catalogues of the Musée Eugène Boudin, 1911
(n° 29), 1959 (n° 90)
R.L Benjamin, *Eugène Boudin*, Paris, 1937, p. 180
R. Schmit, 1973, vol. II, n° 2146

---

*This work breaks with Boudin's habits by
representing the red-skirted women of Berck in
a group and from a distance. In the museum's
collections, this little fisherwoman forms part of
a group that includes small portraits of women
from Honfleur (cat. 62) and Brittany (cat.
73), and a little girl in a straw hat (cat. 67),
all subjects which tied Boudin to the places
that were dear to him.*

88 BRINGING IN THE FISH, ÉTAPLES, c. 1885–1890

Watercolour over dark pencil and charcoal
sketch on beige paper pasted onto paper and
board, 13.5 x 26.8 cm.
Stamped bottom right 'E.B.', with illegible
location and date inscribed in pencil ['Étaples.
80.86'¿]
Illegible annotations in black pencil ['*poisson,
gris*'¿]
Hambourg-Rachet donation, 1988 (Inv. 988-1-5)

Exhibitions
1965 Mairie de Trouville-sur-Mer.
1992 Musée Eugène Boudin and Grenier à Sel,
Honfleur, cat. n° 320

Bibliography
*Donation Hambourg-Rachet au Musée Eugène
Boudin*, 1988, cat. n° 5 (ill. p. 27)

Fisherwoman at Berck
1886

Bringing in the Fish, Étaples
c. 1885–1890
CAT. 88

Waiting on the Shore, Étaples
c. 1885–1890

89 WAITING ON THE SHORE, ÉTAPLES, c. 1885–1890

Watercolour over black pencil and charcoal sketch on beige paper pasted onto paper and board, 13.4 x 26 cm.
Stamped bottom right 'E.B.', illegible annotation in black pencil near lower edge
Hambourg-Rachet donation, 1988
(Inv. 988-1-4)

Exhibition
1992 Musée Eugène Boudin and Grenier à Sel, Honfleur, cat. n° 319

Bibliography
Donation Hambourg-Rachet au Musée Eugène Boudin, 1988, cat. n° 4 (ill. p. 26)

90 WOMEN ON THE BEACH AT BERCK, 1887

Watercolour and highlights of white gouache over graphite pencil sketch on brown paper, 16.7 x 25.5 cm.
Monogram bottom right 'E.B.', location and date bottom left 'Berck 87', graphite pencil annotations bottom right *'Trop vigoureux',* centre right *'sombre'* and top [illegible]
Gift of Professor René Küss, 1989
(Inv. 990-3-1)

Exhibition
1992 Musée Eugène Boudin and Grenier à Sel, Honfleur, cat. n° 322, ill. p. 236

Bibliography
Catalogue of the Musée Eugène Boudin, 1993 (p. 102)
L. Manœuvre, *Eugène Boudin, Dessins,* 1991, p. 58

Women on the Beach at Berck
1887

CAT. 90

RELATED MATERIAL

I ANONYMOUS

Eugène Boudin Painting on the Jetty at Deauville,
June 1896
Ill. p. 142
Photograph pasted onto board
Photograph: 16.5 x 12 cm., board: 18.4 x 13.4 cm.
Dedicated by Boudin below the photograph
'A Georges Sporck. E. Boudin Juin 1896'
Inscribed on the back *'Boudin, le peintre de
marines, dans l'exercice de ses fonctions'*
Gift of Georges Sporck, 1934 (Inv. 934-1-31)

Bibliography
Catalogue of the Musée Eugène Boudin, 1993 (p. 7)
Eugène Boudin, exhibition catalogue, Fondation
Prouvost, Marcq-en-Barœul, 1980.
Y. Le Pichon, *Les Peintres du Bonheur,* Paris, 1983,
p. 78
L'Aube de l'Impressionnisme, exhibition catalogue,
Japan, 1984–1985
B. Bernard, *The Impressionist Revolution,* London,
1986, p. 14
M. Howard, *Monet,* London, 1990
J. P. Crespelle, *Guide de la France Impressionniste,*
1990, Paris, p. 21
M. Kapos, *The Impressionists: a Retrospective,* New
York, 1991
Les Peintres et le Pas-de-Calais, Conseil Général du
Pas de Calais, 1992, p. 123
L. Madeline, *Les Chefs-d'Œuvre de
l'Impressionnisme,* Paris, 1990, p. 85

J. Russel Taylor, *Impressions of France, from Le
Havre to Giverny,* London, 1994, p. 14

II JACQUES DESPIERRE (b. 1912)

Bronze medal, n. d.
Ill. pp. 12, 13
Obverse: *Portrait of Eugène Boudin,* signed bottom
left 'Despierre'
Reverse: *Trois mâts à l'ancre*
Diameter: 70 mm. diameter
Gift of Jacques Despierre, 1974 (Inv. 974-3-1
and 974-3-2)

Exhibition
1992 Musée Eugène Boudin and Grenier à Sel,
Honfleur

III ERNEST-CHARLES GUILBERT (1848–after 1913)

Bust of Eugène Boudin, 1900
Ill. p. 27
Plaster, black patina
Height: 77 cm. Width: 67 cm.
Signed on right side of foot 'E. Guilbert'
On loan from the Ville de Honfleur (Inv. 990-70-1)

IV PAUL HELLEU (1859–1927)

Eugène Boudin Painting on the Jetty at Trouville, 1894
Ill. p. 142
Black and white dry-point engraving
Dimensions of paper: 56 x 34 cm.
Dimensions of engraving: 28 x 20 cm.
Gift of G. Cahen, 1900 (Inv. 900-1-1)

Bibliography

Catalogue of the Musée Eugène Boudin, 1959
(n° 180)
G. Cahen, 1900 (frontispiece)
Trouville et sa Région: Seconde Moitié du XIXe Siècle
(cover ill.), exhibition catalogue, Trouville, 1965

V   LOUIS METTLING (1847–1904)

Portrait of Eugène Boudin

Oil on canvas, 46 x 38 cm.
Unsigned, n.d.
Eugène Boudin bequest, 1899 (Inv. 899-1-66)

Bibliography

Catalogue of the Musée Eugène Boudin, 1911
(n° 111)

Work in poor condition.

VI   HENRI MICHEL-LÉVY (1845–1914)

*The Painter Boudin Painting Animals in the Meadow
at Deauville,* 1880
Ill. p. 136
Oil on canvas, 22 x 27 cm.
Inscribed on the stretcher *'Le peintre Boudin
peignant dans la prairie de Deauville. Juin 1880'*
Eugène Boudin bequest, 1899 (Inv. 899-1-55)

Exhibition

1990–1991 *En Suivant la Touques,* Musée de
Trouville-sur-Mer, 16 November 1990–6 January,
1991, cat. ill. p. 34

Bibliography

Catalogues of the Musée Eugène Boudin, 1911
(n° 104), 1959 (n° 48)
Y. Le Pichon, *Les Peintres du Bonheur,* Paris, 1983,
cat. n° 57

VII   CLAUDE MONET (1840–1926)

*Portrait believed to be of Eugène Boudin working at
Le Havre*
Ill. p. 24
Conté crayon on grey paper, 30 x 22 cm.
Unsigned, n.d.
Gift of Michel Monet, 1956 (Inv. 956-7-2)

Exhibitions

1984–1985 (Japan) Sendai, Sapporo, Tokyo and
Nagoya

Bibliography

Catalogues of the Musée Eugène Boudin, 1959
(n° 130), 1983 (ill. p. 19)
Y. Taillandier, *Monet,* Bruxelles, 1977 (ill. p. 84)
J. Isaacson, *Observation and Reflection, Claude
Monet,* New York, 1978 (ill. p. 26)
J. P. Crespelle, *Guide de la France Impressionniste*
Paris, 1990 (ill. p. 10)
L. Madeline, *Chefs-d'Œuvre de l'Impressionnisme,*
Paris, 1990 (ill. p.85)
Videodisk, Museum Education Consortium,
New York, 1990
S. Patin, *Monet, un Œil, mais, Bon Dieu, quel
Œil!,* Paris, 1991 (ill. p.16)
M. Alphant, *Claude Monet,* Paris, 1992 (ill. p. 71)
J.-J. Lévêque, *Monet,* Paris 1992 (ill. p.18)
J. Welton, *Monet,* London, 1993 (ill. p. 6)

An early work of Monet's.

VIII CHARLES PÉCRUS (1826–1907)

Portrait of Marie-Anne Boudin, 1879
Ill. p. 23
Oil on mahogany panel, 21 x 15.5 cm.
Signed top left 'C. Pécrus 1879'
Eugène Boudin bequest, 1899 (Inv. 899-1-62)

Exhibitions
1899 École Nationale des Beaux-Arts, Paris.
1976–1977 (USA) Northampton and
Williamstown, cat. n° 94, ill. p. 141
1980 Musée de St-Maur-des-Fossés
1989 *Charles Pécrus, du Classicisme à
l'Impressionnisme,* Mairie du 9ᵉ Arrondissement,
Paris, cat. n° 6

Bibliography
Catalogues of the Musée Eugène Boudin, 1911 (n°
124), 1959 (n° 52), 1983 (ill. p.43)

IX ADRIEN VOISARD-MARGERIE (1867–1954)

Portrait of Eugène Boudin

Oil on canvas mounted on board, 41 x 33 cm.
Monogram bottom right 'A.V.M.'
Voisard-Margerie bequest, 1954 (Inv. 954-1-11)

X ANTOINE VOLLON (1833–1900)

Portrait believed to be of Juliette
Ill. p. 26
Oil on panel, 40 x 32 cm.
Signed top left 'A. Vollon'
Inscribed on the back in pencil *'Portrait*

de Juliette' [Juliette Cabaud?]
Eugène Boudin bequest, 1899 (Inv. 899-1-69)

Bibliography
Catalogue of the Musée Eugène Boudin, 1911
(n° 152)

XI EUGÈNE BOUDIN'S EASEL

Ill. p. 80
Polished wood, 138 x 64 cm.
On loan from the Société du Vieux-Honfleur,
1974 (Inv. D. 974-1-1)

Exhibition
1992 Musée Eugène Boudin and Grenier à Sel,
Honfleur, cat. n° 327

XII A PORTFOLIO FORMELY BELONGING TO EUGÈNE BOUDIN

Ill. p. 80
On the top-right corner of the portfolio
is a label marked *'Aquarelle',* and on the left
a label marked '321'. Glued onto the inside
of the folder is a calling-card with the engraved
inscription 'Eugène Boudin' and Boudin's
address, written out by hand 'Trouville–23,
rue Tarole', 36 x 54 cm.
Hambourg-Rachet donation, 1988
(Inv. 988-1-374)

Bibliography
*Donation Hambourg-Rachet au Musée Eugène
Boudin,* 1988, cat. n° 374

XIII Eugène Boudin's Palette, c. 1874

Ill. p. 25
Walnut wood, 43.5 x 32 cm.
Inscribed on the back in white paint
'Une palette d'Eugène Boudin (vers 1874)'
Gift of Jean Fischer, 1974 (Inv. 974-6-1)

Exhibitions
1984–1985 (Japan) Sendai, Sapporo, Tokyo
and Nagoya, cat. n° 17
1985 Salon d'Automne, Grand Palais, Paris,
cat. n° 12 bis
1992 Musée Eugène Boudin and Grenier à Sel,
Honfleur, cat. n° 327

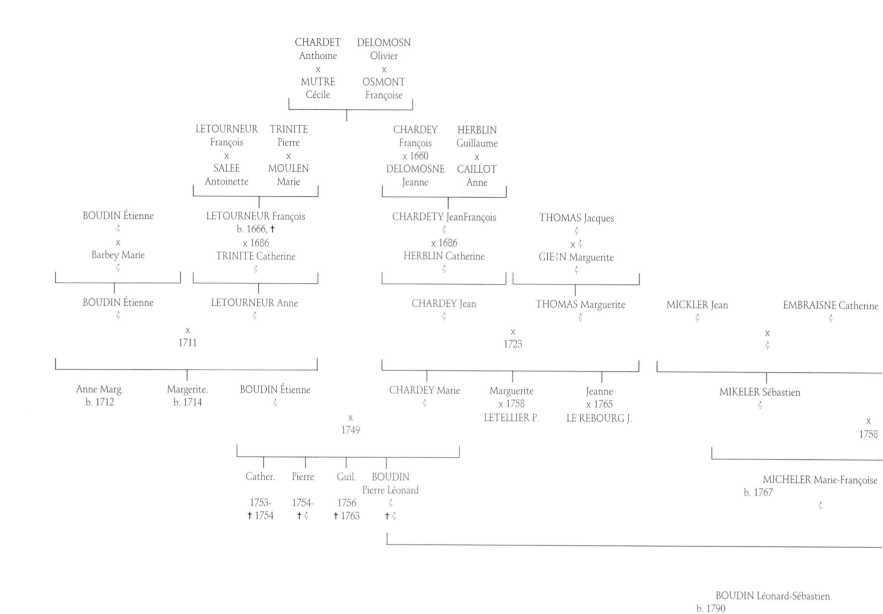

FAMILY TREE

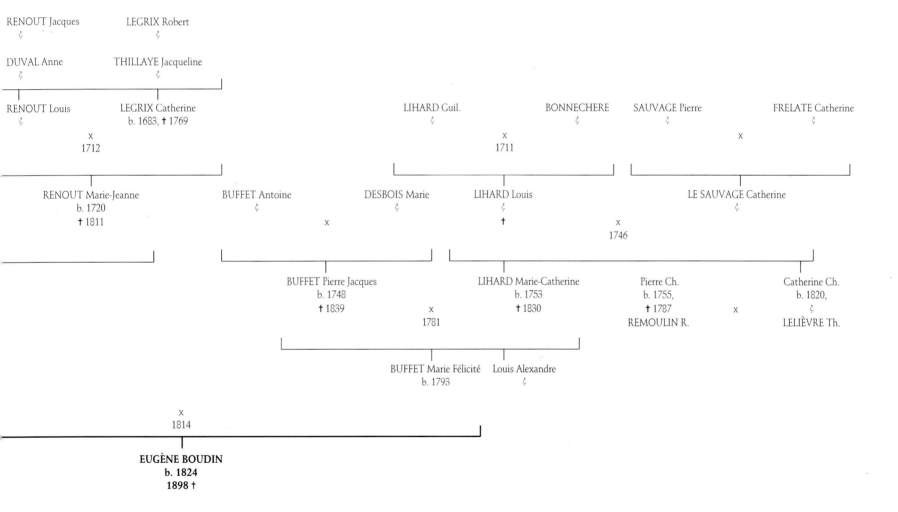

RENOUT Jacques
ç

LEGRIX Robert
ç

DUVAL Anne
ç

THILLAYE Jacqueline
ç

RENOUT Louis
ç

LEGRIX Catherine
b. 1683, † 1769

LIHARD Guil.
ç

BONNECHERE
ç

SAUVAGE Pierre
ç

FRELATE Catherine
ç

x
1712

x
1711

x

RENOUT Marie-Jeanne
b. 1720
† 1811

BUFFET Antoine
ç

DESBOIS Marie
ç

LIHARD Louis
ç

LE SAUVAGE Catherine
ç

x

†

x
1746

BUFFET Pierre Jacques
b. 1748
† 1839

LIHARD Marie-Catherine
b. 1753
† 1830

Pierre Ch.
b. 1755,
† 1787
REMOULIN R.

Catherine Ch.
b. 1820,
ç
LELIÈVRE Th.

x
1781

x

BUFFET Marie Félicité
b. 1793

Louis Alexandre
ç

x
1814

**EUGÈNE BOUDIN
b. 1824
1898 †**

BIBLIOGRAPHY

ALEXANDRE Arsène, Preface to the sale of Eugène Boudin's studio,.Paris, 1899.

BAUDELAIRE Charles, *Oeuvres,* Paris, 1931–1932, 2 vol.

BUHOT Félix, Preface to the exhibition catalogue of 1889.

Bulletin de la Société des Amis du Musée de Honfleur, 1966, 1967, 1968, 1971, 1972–1974, 1975–1977

BURTY Philippe, 'Exposition Boudin', *La République Française,* 8 February, 1883.

CAHEN Gustave, *Eugène Boudin, sa Vie et son Oeuvre,* preface by Arsène Alexandre, Paris, 1900

CARIO Louis, *Eugène Boudin,* Paris, 1928.

COHEN Françoise, *Catalogue des Oeuvres d'Eugène Boudin Conservées au Musée des Beaux-Arts du Havre,* n.d.

DE KNYFF Gilbert, *Eugène Boudin Raconté par lui-même. Sa Vie, son Atelier, son Oeuvre,* Paris, 1976.

DELOUCHE Denise, *Eugène Boudin et la Bretagne,* 1987.

GEFFROY Gustave, 'Eugène Boudin', *La Justice,* 15 February, 1883.

JEAN-AUBRY Gérard, *Eugène Boudin. La vie et l'Oeuvre d'après les Lettres et les Documents Inédits,* Paris, 1922, new ed. Neuchâtel 1968, Paris 1988, with the collaboration of Robert Schmit.

LEMAIRE Solange, 'L'Hostellerie de Saint-Siméon, Berceau de l'Impressionnisme', *Le Pays d'Auge,* 36th year, n° 7, July 1986.

LEMOINE Pascale, *Boudin Roi des Ciels,* Paris, 1981.

MANŒUVRE Laurent, 'Le Peintre Eugène Boudin, la Belgique et les Pays-Bas', *Septentrion, Revue de Culture Néerlandaise,* 1/1987.

MANŒUVRE Laurent, *Eugène Boudin, Dessins,* Paris, 1991.

MANŒUVRE Laurent, *Boudin et la Normandie,* Paris, 1991.

MANŒUVRE Laurent, *Boudin, le Ciel et la Mer,* Paris, 1994.

MELOT Michel, *L'Oeuvre Gravé de Boudin, Corot, Daubigny, Dupré, Jongkind, Millet, Rousseau,* Paris, 1978.

PILLEMENT Georges, *Les pré-Impressionnistes,* Paris, 1975.

REWALD John, *Histoire de l'Impressionnisme,* Paris, 1971, 2 vol.

ROGER-MARX Claude, *Eugène Boudin,* Paris, 1927.

SCHMIT Robert, *Eugène Boudin, Catalogue Raisonné de l'Oeuvre Peint,* Paris, 1973, supp. Paris, 1984, 2nd supp. with Manuel Schmit, Paris, 1993.

SELZ Jean, *Eugène Boudin,* Paris, 1982.

WIZEWA Theodor de, 'Eugène Boudin', *L'Art des Deux Mondes,* 27 December, 1889.

ZOLA Emile, *Salons,* Geneva, 1959.

CATALOGUES OF THE COLLECTIONS AT THE MUSEE EUGENE BOUDIN

1911. LECLERC Léon. Catalogue du Musée

1959. DRIES Jean. Catalogue du Musée

1989. Catalogue de la Donation Hambourg-Rachet

1983, 1988, 1993. BERGERET-GOURBIN Anne-Marie. Catalogue du Musée.

SELECTED EXHIBITIONS, INCLUDING EXHIBITIONS TO WHICH THE MUSEE EUGENE BOUDIN HAS LOANED WORKS BY BOUDIN

1899. *Exposition des Oeuvres d'Eugène Boudin,* Ecole Nationale des Beaux-Arts, Paris, 9–31 January.

1939. Rockefeller Center, New York.

1944. *Marines,* Galerie Charpentier, Paris.

1952. *E. Boudin,* Mairie d'Honfleur. Exhibition organised by the Société des Artistes Honfleurais, July-August, 1952.

1953. *Boudin, Jongkind, Dubourg,* Mairie d'Honfleur. Exhibition organised by the Société des Artistes Honfleurais, 19 July-30 August.

1956. *Les Boudin du Musée Municipal de Honfleur,* Galerie Katia Granoff, Paris, 10 November–8 December.

1957. *Charles Baudelaire,* Bibliothèque Nationale, Paris.

1958. *Jongkind, Boudin,* Galerie Lucien Blanc, Aix-en-Provence, July.
   Trésors du Musée de Caen, Galerie Charpentier, Paris.

1958–1959. *Boudin,* Marlborough Fine Art, London, November–January.

1964. *Eugène Boudin en Bretagne,* Musée des Beaux-Arts, Rennes, 1 February–15 March.

1965. *Trouville, Seconde Moitié du XIXè Siècle: Boudin, Pécrus,* Mairie de Trouville-sur-Mer, 10 July–16 August.
   Boudin, Aquarelles et Pastels, Musée du Louvre, Paris.

1966. Galerie Max Kaganovitch, Paris.

1970–1971. *Impressionnist Art,* Leningrad, 1 December–10 January.
   Moscow, 25 January–1 March.
   Madrid, 15 March–10 April.

1976–1977. *Jongkind and the pre-Impressionists: Painters of the École St-Siméon,* Smith College Museum of Art, Northampton, 15 October–5 December,
   Clark Art Institute, Williamstown, 17 December–13 February.

1978. *Le Paysage Normand dans la Littérature et dans l'Art,* Musée de l'Ancien Evêché, Evreux, 22 March–7 May.
    Sur les Pas d'Eugène Boudin et E. Boudin dans les Collections, Musée des Beaux-Arts, Le Havre, 15 September–4 December.

1979. *Eugène Boudin,* Kunsthalle, Bremen, 23 September–4 November.

1980. *Charles Pécrus,* Musée de St Maur-des-Fossés, 19 January–8 March.
   Eugène Boudin, Fondation Prouvost, Marcq-en-Baroeul, 9 February–11 May.

1982. *L'Art dans les provinces de France,* Société des Artistes Français, Grand Palais, Paris, 8–31 May.

1983. *Dans la Lumière de Corot,* Fondation Prouvost, Marcq-en-Baroeul, 28 January–24 April.

1984-1985, 'The Dawn of Impressionism', Japan.
   Sendai, 23–28 October.
   Sapporo, 13–18 November.
   Tokyo, 15–27 January.
   Nagoya, 8–13 February.

1985. *Aux Sources de l'Impressionnisme,* Salon d'Automne, Grand Palais, Paris, 16 October–3 November.

1987–1988. *Eugène Boudin, Dessins Inédits,* Musée d'Orsay, Paris, 26 October–25 January.

1988. *Monet and his Friends,* Museum of Modern Art, Ibaraki (Japan), 1 October–6 November.
   Esquisses Peintes, Moments Anonymes. Normandie 1850–1950, Musée des Beaux-Arts, Caen, 11 June–26 September.

1989. *Eugène Boudin,* Musée Municipal de l'Evêché, Limoges, July–August.

1990–1991. *En suivant la Touques,* Musée de Trouville, 16 November, 1990–6 January, 1991.

1991. *Honfleur avant l'Impressionnisme,* Musée Eugène Boudin, Honfleur, 6 July–30 September.

1992. *Eugène Boudin,* Musée Eugène Boudin and Grenier à Sel, Honfleur, 11 April–12 July.

1992–1993. *Boudin at Trouville,* Glasgow Art Gallery and Museum, 20 November–28 February.

1993. *Eugène Boudin, le Trait, la Touche, la Tache,* Hôtel de Ville, Aulnay-sous-Bois, 15 November–12 December.

1996. *Eugène Boudin, Prelude to Impressionism,* Museum of Fine Arts, Rio de Janeiro, 11 June–6 August.

1996–1997. *Eugène Boudin and the Painters at Honfleur,* Japan.
   Bunkamura Museum of Art, Tokyo, 12 October–8 December.
   Prefectural Museum of Art, Tsu, 9, 12 December, 1996–2 February.
   Mito Museum of Modern Art, Ibaraki, 8 February–28 March.

Index of names

Page numbers in italics refer to illustrations.

Index of works by Eugène Boudin

Lay-out: Ariane Aubert
Editing: Véronique Le Dosseur/Somogy Editions d'Art

Photographic credits:
Henri Brauner/Musée Eugène Boudin, Honfleur
Agence photographique de la Réunion des Musées Nationaux: p. 32, p. 34
Réunion des Musées Nationaux–Jean Schorman: p. 36
Musée de Caen/Martine Seyve: p. 38, p. 40

ISBN 2–85056–265–3
Printed in Italy

Copyright registration: fourth quarter 1996

Photoengraving: Fotolito Star, Grassobbio, Italy
Camera-ready copy: GPI, Juigné-sur-Sarthe
Printed in November 1996 on the presses of Grafedit, Azzano San Paolo, Italy